9/7/23

THE LAST REAL IMMIGRANT

FROM OLD WORLD ROOTS TO NEW WORLD OPPORTUNITIES

BY JOSEPH GALLIANI

First Printing: June 2023

ISBN Hard Cover: 978-1-961074-01-9
Soft Cover: 978-1-961074-02-6

Printed in the USA

Publisher: Holland Robinson Publishing

Cover Design: Boss Media

Interior Design and Layout: Boss Media

For more information, please visit www.hollandrobinsonpublishing.com or contact info@hollandrobinsonpublishing.com.

To Dad. For his everlasting presence and inspiration.

TABLE OF CONTENTS

AUTHOR'S NOTE

As I write this book, I feel that I have lived a blessed yet somewhat laborious life, not-withstanding many of the obstacles that have always been around me. They made me a better man. But if it weren't for my father's teachings, I would have tripped and fallen as I encountered many of those obstacles. This is my first, and possibly my last, book that I would contemplate writing; too many years in the making. I want to make it my best. After all, my credentials are in the IT profession, but that technology never changed me and who I am. It just made me aware that without culture, respect, and hard work, you don't achieve higher grounds.

The upcoming one-hundred years of our history in this book, which is well entrenched in my family, is my legacy to it. I wasn't aware at a very young age that because of my father, I would be catapulted on a journey that would take me across three continents. As a naturalized American now, I have a much wider perspective and understanding of this wonderful world, but America tops it all. How I wrote this book is just as if I am conversing with you, the reader. I learned at an early age that balanced and fact-driven communications bring every one of us together. It makes us understand who we are, where we come from, and where we want to go. My dialogued stories, hopefully, will flow naturally from this paper to your soul.

I want to thank all my readers for their support, and I invite you to provide your honest feedback. We really need to make our time here as productive as it can be. Every line of work is important no matter what you do. My father, to whom this book is dedicated, worked with his hands but was guided by his incredible, logical intellect and often idealistic mind. He accomplished all that he could during his tenure. I ask all of you to remain engaged and proactive in everything that you aspire to do. If "The Last Real Immigrant" did it, I believe that you can also accomplish it. Hopefully, this book will guide you to undertake this task.

–Joseph Galliani

INTRODUCTION

As we currently navigate through these highly charged political times, this book addresses the history and the experiences of an immigrant family. This book accounts a family history that isn't entirely mine but could represent a shared past, full of sacrifices but involving accomplishments too. The story of my family took place during one of the last waves of the European migration to America. This book starts in the country where it all began for us: the North African land of Libya, which was once a thriving Italian colony.

Apart from the vast history of Italy, it is interesting to remember that Libya benefited from the introduction of both the modern European irrigation systems and home-building techniques. From 1910 to 1946, colonial Italy worked hard to bring Libya out of the "middle ages" and imprinted some of its cultures on the various Arab nations. My family members, all Italian citizens, unfortunately, migrated back to Italy, our homeland, in the late 1950s as Libya started to show signs of internal monarchy government deterioration and financial uncertainties. Living in Italy in the 1960s, we experienced part of the country's many financial instabilities and trying times. During those years, many groups of skilled Italians seized the risks, looking for more opportunities, and immigrated to their final destination: The United States of America. Reading this book, Americans can re-experience the 1960s and 1970s and rejoice that once upon a time, America implemented Immigration Laws to benefit American growth and security.

This book recounts not only my personal history but also that of my family meeting the requirements and rules of the American immigration system of the 1960s era. Thus, this work analyzes how the "merit system" worked then - and should still work today - representing, in my opinion, the only correct approach to enriching our country with immigrants that bring skills, hard work, and vision. If we look back to this period, those immigrants have accelerated the growth, the economy, the presence, and the strength of the United States in the world. That progress was accomplished by taking a bilateral approach: on the one hand, by integrating with the American philosophy; on the other by keeping their own culture, a parameter to achieve greatness and prosperity. Nowadays, dealing with the current immigration circumstances, one should look back and reevaluate the use of the functioning process used in those times to enter America.

This book is divided into three parts. The first one I call "Out of Africa." It details and describes my family's roots and life in Northern Africa. It starts in the 1950s in Tripoli, the capital city of Libya, and contains many references to our earlier historical generational epochs. It is undeniable that each family has their own origins. The history of mine is not for the fainthearted: it carried joy and sorrow as we fought to establish our identity and history. The challenges also established the concepts and guidelines for our early successes and, unfortunately, also some disappointments too. Coming from far and exotic places where only a few thrived and endured in spite of everything, my family blossomed and prospered, especially when we got to America. With each experience, though, the body, the mind, and the character became a gateway to challenge the future with each of the previously obtained lessons.

The second part, titled "Out of Italy," highlights our family's early accomplishments and proficiencies that catapulted us to where we are and live today. It takes place in 1960s Italy, a time of new discoveries and peace but one that demands hard work. It shaped the skin and principles of the family and our early contributions guided by an entrenched work ethic. It explains how respect, hard work, and education go hand in hand to achieve one's goals. As Italians with a rich millennial history, we struggled with the system and government of those ages. By the early 1960s, World War II had long since ended for the Italian population. However, it still carried with it a heavy burden of reconstruction for all European citizens.

Ingenuity carried Italians through time, even before Christ engraved our genetic heritage. The great minds who lived in all the different countries of Europe have contributed their culture, art, intellect, and working principles to create the great "melting pot" represented by the United States of America.

The last part of the book I call "Coming to America" covers almost half of this book's content. It narrates, with sometimes unpolished realities, our American experiences starting with our arrival in the late 1960s to the present day. By reading the substance and some of the stories and events that took place, especially during the early days of our entry into the country and those early years, you can realize some of the burdens and sacrifices that awaited every immigrant family. Baby Boomers or Generation X may find solace in reading and recalling some of these events from decades past in America. I strongly recommend this book to Millennials since it may reinforce in them the traditional views and expectations of their parents. My real-life illustrations, family experiences, and trials throughout all three parts of this book should convey what immigration can achieve by using my family as an example. Earlier American immigration laws were not perfect by any means, but they produced and gathered the correct effect in shaping the last century of our American past.

If history is to be studied, we must learn from it, not reject it. It is evident that our country, in this current era, does not truly look at the past or is somewhat disengaged in identifying the accomplishments and endeavors of this nation's record.

It is important to remember that most immigrants entered the U.S. by qualifying for entry based on immigration laws, which seemed or were, partially defective. Despite that, in most cases, they achieved the intended outcome. Looking at our nation today, we can notice that the immigrants of the past century have made substantial contributions to global prominence in the international scenario of the USA. Unfortunately, our country's immigration system currently operates on an untested and logistics-less basis.

We are experiencing a new wave of unfettered immigration.

Legitimately skilled immigrants of the past and their families have contributed heart and soul to America's past and future. Their impact has also shaped our country into the ultimate economic and military power in the world. Uninhibited and unregulated immigration, for the most part, does not bear many fruits or skills or bring progress to our nation to meet our future needs.

A reflection on the topic is, therefore, needed. Should our government allow entry to everyone who wants to enter and live in our country? Do we want an open borders nation? What about those who came, sometimes waiting for years, vetted by American ideology and laws of those early days, presenting merits, skills, and a guarantor before being allowed to reside here? Should our immigrant class be exasperated by what my family and I had to endure and engage in? My father, the patriarch of my family, sacrificed a lot and had to prove much, sometimes working endless hours. The journey of my family's history is about to start: would you be able to assimilate into this rich immigrant-centered American history? You will be the ultimate judge.

My family and I have adapted to our new life in America with its customs, foods, and work ethics, and, as you will discover through the reading, the stories depicted bring this book to life. My experiences and that of my family - that maybe, at the end of this book, will become a little bit of yours too - are about to be presented. As your eyes read the pages, you will assume the arduous role of critic, judge, and the final advocate. At the end of the reading, you will surely be able to answer the questions you encounter.

The Last Real Immigrant. That is how I decided to title my book. But what if it is not really the last?

The Last Real Immigrant

OUT OF AFRICA

One of my most vivid and fond recollections takes me back to my early pre-teen days -- it keeps reiterating and shimmering in my mind. Here I am, lying down on one of those old-fashioned beach folding chairs. If you were born fifty years ago, you may remember or have owned one of them, the ones made of aluminum tubing with plastic colorful strings wrapped from side to side for support. It was one of those countless sunny, hot, and lazy summer afternoons on our small veranda off the first-floor apartment of a four-story condominium complex.

It is the mid-1960s, 1966 to be exact; I am living in Messina, a somewhat large suburban city on the coast of northern Sicily. I am just about eleven years old, the eldest child in my family. Most of the non-working people in the city are taking their afternoon nap. In Mexico and South America, they call it a "Siesta," very much also practiced in this southern part of the Italian country. During these hours, most of the city stores are closed and reopen at 5:00 PM in the summer months since most people are not out shopping due to the afternoon's heat. Looking back at this ritual, it is striking to realize today how simple and carefree everyday life was back then for me. I experience a nostalgic passion recollecting those times. I lived in a time when life was so unpretentious and purely cultural, unaffected by political views; it was a gift to my youth. I did not realize what a golden time that was when I compare it with my current life today. Not that I am currently struggling, it was just a carefree time, and it should have been that, after all, I was not even a teenager yet.

My father, at that time, was working in a shipyard located in the city of Messina, where they built the hydrofoils; these boats delivered advanced high-speed transportation on the sea and eventually made their way to many faraway places such as the Nile River and large European lakes. These hydrofoils were considered unique - then manufactured right there in the Messina shipyard since their initial launch in the mid-1950s. I will explain what a hydrofoil is and its details later in this book. I will also express much about my father's work and other circumstances, together with his travels to foreign countries on behalf of this hydrofoil builder.

My mother was a homemaker and a caring wife who, on most of those summer afternoons, would be busy knitting or altering our family clothing. She would do all this while keeping an eye on the family dinner simmering on the kitchen stove. During this time, my sister and my brother, having been four and seven years younger than me, respectively, were expected to take their afternoon nap notwithstanding their objections. This routine was in place during those long days of the summer months. The afternoon nap refreshed them so that they would not be cranky for dinner or during the early night hours. There was a quietness all around our neighborhood during those summer afternoons. The open veranda in our apartment faced the city street, but it was rarely noisy during those afternoons. Very few Italians could afford a car in those years, and even fewer would use it if they had one unless it was necessary. Gasoline, which was sold by the liter, was very expensive. The maintenance of the car and other financial factors kept its use to a minimum. The few families that could afford a car would use it mostly on Sundays and holidays to take their family to the countryside or the beach, especially during the summer. It was more likely to see a Vespa or a motorbike driving by our apartment than a car. However, when I would hear the distinguished sound of a car engine approaching, I would lean my head up from my chair and look over the balcony rail to see what kind of car drove by. This was just one more reason to be out on the balcony and to be somewhat entertained. I would try to identify the person driving it and also possibly identify the make and model of that car. It is natural for a young boy to be curious and assertive at that age. Remember, the Internet was nowhere to be found, nor had anyone even thought of it. The few television sets that were owned by very few people had no programs broadcast during the afternoons. Nonetheless, what really kept me interested during those days was reading the daily national newspaper or weekly magazines and reading about the Vietnam War.

You must wonder what an eleven-year-old boy living in Italy is doing reading about the Vietnam War in 1966. After all, I was thousands of miles away from America, and Vietnam was also on the other side of the world. I was interested in reading what the American media was reporting on the casualties incurred that week by the American army. I would feverishly look at the headcount of their enemy, the Vietcong, and North Vietnam. I was cheering to make sure that the Americans were inflicting at least twice or three times their losses to the enemy. At that young age, you cannot ascertain what it means to die or be wounded during a war. When you are eleven or twelve years old, you do not understand death quite like when you are an adult. You are obscured by the agony and grief of losing someone very close to you. Death was seen transparently, just like in the American movies of the cowboys and Indians together with the war movies of those times. The John Wayne and Frank Sinatra war movies of the 1950s and 60s did not convey what war was really all about. It was a clever way to cheer for the Americans without understanding that even one American death was too much of a loss. The families that suffered any loss during the Vietnam War were not in my mind. I just wanted the Americans to win no matter what, and I did not understand the human cost of that war. I was also fascinated to read that the Air Force was bombing the North Vietnam country and inflicting heavy damage with many casualties to that enemy. I guess that at my age, with little experience and still developing a mindset, I looked at this war, not from a human loss perspective.

However, why did I have so much interest in the Vietnam War? The main reason was that my father, Giorgio, often spoke to me about the Americans in many of our conversations. He endowed their greatness and good-heartedness to being very fair people. "You know," he used to say to me, "They call them the Yankees that won WWII, which brought democracy and freedom to the world." But why could my father speak so positively and know so much about the American people? Well, my father lived his youth in Libya, a North African country. He became familiar with the American culture and history because there was a large presence of American forces in that country, and remained there even after the Second World War. Their presence was mainly concentrated within a very large Air Force base in the capital city of Tripoli. While living there, he was able to interact with them and actually worked at the American Air Base, which I will cover later in this portion of the book. He instilled in me the respect and the power that Americans projected to other nations of the world. This became his conviction from his interactions with them during all the years that he lived in Tripoli. This was a somewhat favorite subject between us to discuss as I was growing up and long thereafter. The daily news about the Vietnam War was a big deal in Italy in those days since WWII was still fresh on everyone's mind. This also made a lot of sense because America freed Italy from Fascism. The Americans were now trying to accomplish the same for the South Vietnamese people being ruled by a Communist regime in the North.

This is where we will start our short "**Out of Africa**" section of this book.

But, we must first go back to a time before I was born when my father was in his teens and a child of Italian parents. My father grew up and spent his childhood and early adult life in Tripoli, the capital of Libya. His father, Giuseppe, lived in Tripoli and was a homebuilder during the earlier Italian colonial days before the Second World War. You may ask how Libya became an Italian colony. History tells us that in 1911, Italian troops invaded the Turkish province of Libya (then part of the Ottoman Empire) and started the Italo-Turkish War. As a result, Italian Tripolitania and Italian Cyrenaica were established, later unified in the colony of Libya.

Perhaps the most important reason for Italy to colonize Libya was nationalism. Italy saw Libya and other countries of Northern Africa as part of the old Roman Empire that rightfully belonged to Italy. By colonizing, they were just returning these countries to the empire where they belonged. This reasoning was not an acceptable way to carry out this outdated thinking. Unfortunately, it is still a reason for other countries like Russia to try to re-acquire their lost regions during the dissolution of the Soviet Union.

My father was the only son and grew up in this foreign land of Libya. To those not familiar with the country of Libya, the brief history of this country is that it is located on the northern coast of Africa facing the Mediterranean Sea. This body of water spans about 100 miles north up to the island of Sicily. Libya gained its independence from Italy in 1951 after World War II. The United States was influential in setting up a new government and appointed diplomats to guide its postwar planning. In 1943, President Franklin D. Roosevelt began a new policy toward Libya. He opposed plans for further European agricultural settlements since he believed that Libya should be independent. Libya was used by Italy as an agricultural colonial settlement before the war together with their two other colonies. For the avid historian, the two other Italian colonies in North Africa were Somalia and Ethiopia. This was analogous to the English and French having also colonized other parts of Africa and the world. At the 1945 Potsdam Conference, President Harry Truman declined to take a trusteeship for Libya, and in 1949 the

United States supported a U.N. resolution for Libyan independence. Even before Libya achieved independence in 1951, Washington started an aid program emphasizing badly needed secondary education, English language, and vocational training. While foreign government aid was desperately needed during this period, by the 1960s it was dwarfed in economic importance by the investments and training programs of foreign oil companies in this region, especially that of American oil companies. This is when American companies, together with some European companies, found large deposits of oil reserves in this part of the world. *(Taken From Middle East Institute paragraph 1319 18th St. NW, Washington D.C. 2003.)* However, before this oil discovery in the 1960s, the Americans, post-World War II, rehabilitated many infrastructures in Libya. This included a very large Air Force base in Tripoli called Wheelus.

Wheelus Air Base was originally constructed by the Italian Air Force in 1923 and was known as Mellaha Air Base. This base was substantially damaged during the war but was rebuilt and improved by the United States to be used by its Air Force as a point of operation in Libya due to its strategic location on the shores of the Mediterranean. It is a well-known historical fact that, at one time, this was the largest U.S. military facility outside of the United States. It had an area of twenty square miles along the seacoast of Tripoli. The base had a beach club, the largest military hospital outside of the U.S., a multiplex cinema, a bowling alley, and a high school for 500 students. The base also had a radio and TV station and a shopping mall together with fast food outlets. At its height, it had over 15,000 military personnel and their dependents living there. Today the facility is called Mitiga International Airport in Tripoli.

During our many political chats, especially during my high school and college days, my father would tell me stories about his time living in Libya. He would also go into detail about the airport runways at that base. According to his recollection, they dwarfed most of today's larger commercial airports; he said they seemed "endless." But sometimes, with a sad tone of his voice, he would mention how the Americans one day decided to leave and relinquish their use of this large Air Force base in Tripoli. During the later Coup that led Muammar Qaddafi to take control of the country of Libya, this base became a center for the dictator's military projects. The amount of work and money that the Americans invested in building and maintaining this base was astronomical by the standards back then. My father described to me that one day the Americans just packed up and left it all behind. If any of my readers are familiar with our American history around the world, you can corroborate how well we are recognized for spending outrageous amounts of money in many foreign countries. This is attributed to the many political doctrines that have been implemented by all the different administrations of our past in Washington, D.C. From my perspective, America has always been willing to accommodate and build many projects around the world with the justification of having a military interest. Unfortunately, many of these became a massive waste of money, which the taxpayers of the United States had to endure, and we still are. Very few of them were of any use to our world interest, and most of them were short-sighted. I am not going to speculate or suggest that many of these projects were not beneficial, but in hindsight, we could have done a much better job with our taxpayers' dollars. I will leave this ideology discussion to the many of you that may have much more experience than me in foreign politics. My only contention here is that the United States keeps repeating this same error without having any real cultural understanding, especially in the Middle East, as we have all witnessed in our past decades' disasters and again in the last few years.

That must have been a very sad day for my father when he found out that the Americans just left that beautiful, strategic, and expensive Air Force base behind. My father always thought that if it wasn't for that opportunity to work at the Air Force base in his 20s, he wouldn't have been able to gain experience in advancing his mechanical skills. This was the start of his professional life as he became, through the years, an accomplished and respected master diesel engine mechanic. It didn't matter to him what kind of machine he worked on, a car engine, truck, or heavy equipment; he could rebuild an old engine without any books or guidelines, following the manufacturer's basic specifications and his acquired skills. When it came to small powerboats or motorcycle engines, he considered them like small toys to play around with. Throughout his life, just to bring some relationships into perspective, my father also worked on massive commercial ocean ships' engines, where just their engine crankshaft measured over thirty feet long.

My father did not attend high school since the educational infrastructure was almost non-existent in those days, especially in Tripoli. He was a young teenager during the Second World War and witnessed some of the American aerial bombings and just barely escaped death many times. Since he was very young, he couldn't join the Italian army, and I am very glad of that because he may have been killed, and I would not be here writing this book. When the war was over, he found himself in Libya and did not go back to school. One of his father's friends in Tripoli owned an automotive repair shop in the city. The owner took my father under his wing and taught him how to repair automobile car engines and all the other skills that come with it. He worked diligently for over two years at this shop. He started when he was fifteen or sixteen years old, working with no pay as this was the standard way in those days since the owner allowed you to learn a trade. The owner of the repair shop invested his time to teach you the secrets and skills of the trade, and you would repay him with your free labor. During those several years of personal sacrifice, my father picked up a lot of knowledge and experience and loved working on engines. Somehow, my father had that inherited gift in his genes to take apart broken mechanical things like auto engines and other mechanical gear. He would fix them or rebuild them with new parts and put them back together in proper working order. His father Giuseppe, since he was a homebuilder, had made many acquaintances, and some of them were prominent people in Tripoli. One of those individuals told him that the Americans were looking for good mechanics at the Air Force base in Tripoli. He suggested to him that "from what I have seen, your son Giorgio is very good with his hands in fixing cars and could also learn the English language very fast." This person introduced my father to the maintenance shop manager in charge of hiring at the American military base.

A few days later my father was hired by the Americans as one of their base mechanics. The job required working with the repair crews for the trucks, cars, and jeeps, keeping them in top running condition for the military. He could not have found a better opportunity to put his skills to work and the additional pleasure of working for the Americans. He eventually learned enough broken English to get by and he flourished and gained much experience up to the day when the base was finally closed. During this time at the base, my father made many friends. He was also able to experience firsthand the American military ideologies: personal honesty and dedication to their work. He explained to me many times that he was astonished by the amount of resources that the American Air Force had; they had so much equipment and spare parts at their disposal. He alleged how they were a powerhouse compared with many other nations, especially in that part of the world. He recounted many times to me that he witnessed the American crews just replacing a failed engine with a brand new one, not even checking to see if the failed engine could be repaired. The American way of thinking was to fix it fast and put it back in operational status as soon as possible. It also was their way of making sure that the equipment was reliable in swapping the whole unit with a brand new one; it just made sense for them as a result. You can get a feel for this mentality today, the way the General Motors and

Fords of the world came to be America's economic, corporate powerhouses. The other main reason, not even remotely available to any other world countries, was an endless flow of money and resources from the U.S. government. After all, this was the United States Air Force. No expense was too great for the American government other than taking care of their military forces and especially their Air Force personnel. I am afraid that this is still the case, which is acceptable as long as we can afford it. The last time I studied some of these large military and financial aid expenditures, it was obvious to me that we were not getting much return on our investments. We largely justify it as an investment in world security. This justification makes everyone feel good about it, but it may not be the truth when you break down the components.

As my father interacted with many people at the Air Force base, he also took advantage of some of the benefits available at the base, like smoking American cigarettes, which cost much less and were hardly available anywhere else in town. I never really saw my father as an American cowboy smoking cigarettes; he reminded me more of a Marlon Brando on his custom motorcycle. During the weekends when he was free, he would earn some extra money by driving some of the influential personnel at the base on short game hunting trips to the nearby desert. My father knew his way around the city periphery and the close hunting grounds from his younger days living in that part of the country. Some of this socializing with the American brass helped him in getting to know people, sometimes getting some preferred treatment when needed and great references on his behalf.

At the age of twenty in 1951, my father already owned an American Jeep that he bought at the so-called American base scrap yard. I am sure that the Jeep was not much of a scrap; it just needed some hard work and sweat, and by replacing some parts, it was back in running condition, just like new. The city of Tripoli was also home to some British citizens that elected to stay behind and live there after the war. He befriended a few of them and, together with the Americans, they would go out to the city dance clubs or meet at the local bars. My father was never much of a drinker. I think he would rather hang around the bar, maybe having a soda, smoking a cigarette, and possibly practicing his broken English in a spirited conversation.

One thing that stands out to my understanding of those days was his hobby of dirt bike motorcycle racing. Here is why I make my reference to him as more of a Marlon Brando than a John Wayne. Like in the Brando film "The Wild One," my father resembled that figure to me; he was just a maverick during those days with his motorcycle. He had all the tools, parts, knowledge, and a garage so that he could fix his toys after work. I have photos of him racing in a dirt road circuit with his own rebuilt BSA off-road motorcycle.

My father Giorgio in action in one of those races.

He joined a club of motorcycle enthusiasts that would compete during the weekends a couple of times a month among themselves on the hastily marked dirt road circuit just to prove their skills and probably score some macho points. He told me that he recalled that three English and two American racing aficionados were part of this motorcycle club. These races were organized by a local enthusiast group. The motorcyclists in this group would compete, and my father was one of them. There were small prizes for the winner, maybe a trophy, but the competition was mainly done for self-accomplishment and bragging rights. I do not know how well he did, but I remember him telling me about one racer: an English fellow with his Norton motorcycle. He was very daring and sometimes dangerous to others on the course. You had to be sure that you kept your distance until you could overtake him. The word was that he would try to cut you off, especially if you were approaching a curve to try to pass him. He said one other driver riding a Triumph, a very fast motorcycle, unfortunately, lacked the skills of a good driver. He could not handle his motorcycle and would attempt very daring and hazardous maneuvers on the course, sometimes causing accidents.

One of my aunts, my mother's sister, told me that she believed that was how my father met my mother during one of these racing events. In those days, there was not much going on for outdoor entertainment, maybe going to the movie theater, a circus if it was in town, or a club if you belonged to it. I believe that my future mother was watching one of these motorcycle racing events. Since my mother was very young then, maybe sixteen, she would go there with her older first cousins that also lived in Tripoli. During one of these races, my father hit a bad part of the dirt road, maybe a small hole or uneven ground, and he lost control of the motorcycle. He fell and hit the ground as his motorcycle skidded with him since he let it go in order not to be injured by his own motorcycle. I guess he found himself rolling on the pavement and scraping a few parts of his body, especially since he was not wearing full protective clothing. Who could afford that back then, anyways? A few local spectators watching the event right at the side of the road came to his aid.

My mother and her cousins also approached the incident scene to see what they could do to help. My future mother, Rosa, recognized this fallen racer upon arriving at the scene. This was because Giorgio's father, Giuseppe, had done business with Rosa's father, Vincenzo. From what I learned about this event, my mother recognized him because a few days earlier, he had driven his father in his American Jeep to her house to meet her father. The reason for that meeting was that Vincenzo wanted to build a small garage on his property to store some of his agricultural equipment. He asked Giuseppe to give him an estimate to build that garage. I guess when a young "Giorgio" pulls up to your home driving an American Jeep in those days, it was hard to forget.

The girls, including my mother, helped my father up from his fall and provided water for cleaning the scratches and bruises; my father was done racing for that day. However, for the reader, my father would be back many more times racing with the English and the American boys. As far as my mother goes, I guess they started to see each other after this unfortunate or real fortunate event. The two families also shared a mutual culture and interests, from a motorcycle accident to a newfound relationship that would span from then on for over fifty years. I will follow up on this newfound love relationship and their wedding in the upcoming section.

America played a crucial role in helping many other foreign countries after the war. Some of them produced positive results, while others went by unnoticed, and some were even counterproductive. The Libya story, for my part, was a positive result, especially for my father since he recognized and witnessed the accomplishments of the Americans in Tripoli. It etched in my father certain positive recognitions of them that would become a beacon for his life and our family's future.

Returning now to when I was reading the world news events from that balcony in 1966 about the Vietnam War and of the Americans dying there, the source of these interests from my perspective and history may be slightly clearer now: it was my father's early life experiences and upbringing that entered me into that curious love affair with the United States. He exposed me to his interactions with the Americans, which left an idealistic imprint on me. Obviously, the most important reason, as we all know, for the Vietnam War was that America was defending her principles of Democracy. While I still think that Democracy works well for some countries to govern their people, it doesn't mix well in some parts of the world. The reason why this fails is because their culture and way of thinking may need to be modified in order to evolve to today's realities. Unfortunately, many of these populations in the world have been oppressed by tyrannical leaders that came to power because their citizens either chose to ignore or were not interested in retaining basic human liberties. The oppression via harsh and sometimes deadly means was protracted and eventually became their way of life.

In our America, the colonists finally realized that they would not live under English colonial rule because they valued their civil liberties. We fought with our hearts and souls, and many people died in this fight, but we eventually became independent through our Revolution to forge our own independent path. Even if our current government is not a Democracy, but a Republic, it is very close to an ideal freedom-loving society. Our Republic overlaps many of the Democratic principles where the people are in charge of their own destiny in very simple terms.

The Vietnam War was a war of principles, but unfortunately, it was our principles and those of the same South Vietnamese. They did not want to be ruled by a dictatorial northern Vietnamese government that wanted to force their communist rule over the southern portion of that country. Americans, like most of us, are brought up during their youth to always try to help the disadvantaged ones if they are able to. Thus, when Americans became aware of the circumstances happening in Vietnam and considering we were fresh out of a big war, it became a matter of principle to help other countries from being occupied by a dictatorial ruling society. We mean well, but other cultures do NOT respond well, as we have seen time and time again, even in the last few decades or so. Every country needs to go through its own process to find its own identity, just like we did with our American Revolution. I must say that it did not end there. Our individual freedoms are challenged almost every day. Each of us must stand firm to these challenges and defend them just like our ancestors did. The human traits of some of our elected representatives, at times, get out of check. These elected individuals that rise to power become so overtaken by their ego trip that they forget what they were elected to do and try to impose restrictions or try to limit their own citizens' God-given liberties. This is when WE THE PEOPLE need to step up for our rights and fight any of these attempts to limit or take away any of our Constitutional rights. I would like to emphasize here that this is the story of an immigrant family that identifies very much with the American Constitution. This book is just the accounting of very laborious and sometimes hard-to-swallow events from an immigrant's, now a naturalized American Citizen's, point of view.

I would like to continue now with our history and life in Libya. It may be a little unusual, but not far-fetched by any means. In the 1950s, many Italians remained behind from the post-war days to help in aiding the local people in that nation's rebuilding process. The Italians were able to maintain their Italian citizenship, which was recognized by their home country. They were welcomed to stay if they wished by the newly created independent monarch government of Libya after the war. Italy had lost the war and also lost their colonies, but the Italian culture - the one that goes back thousands of years - was not lost during the Second World War, not to mention a hard lesson from the fascist experience. The Italians that lived from and on this land worked together with the newly instituted Libyan government to bring the country out of a primarily agricultural economy. Libya needed to compete in the new world standard, and energy – specifically oil - was the new standard. This would not come to play, as I mentioned before, until the early 1960s when the American and European oil companies discovered large oil reserves in Libya.

It is my perspective that knowing some facts about the countries that have been written about brings the reader closer to understanding the history and the processes. In this instance, it is worthwhile to mention that today the oil reserves in Libya are one of the largest, if not the largest, in Africa and among the ten largest globally, with 46.4 billion barrels as of 2010. Oil production was 1.65 million barrels per day as of 2010, giving Libya 77 years of reserves at current production rates if no new reserves were to be found. Thus, as we can assert, Libya could be one of the richest countries in the world if it wasn't for some of the radical groups that brought this country today to its knees. These forces and groups were contained when Muammar Qaddafi, the country's ruler and self-appointed dictator from 1969 to 2011, remained in control. Unfortunately, this control was lost when Mr. Qaddafi was killed mostly by an American campaign designed to get rid of some of the world's worst dictators. America, in my opinion, played a hefty and devastating role by bringing instability to Libya and the whole region with our thinking that "We know better and what is good for you." We failed to recognize that the cultures that have been there for thousands of years have an embedded infrastructure, rules, and, disciplines that carried them through the ages. We mean well most of the time and try to bring freedom and democracy to foreign countries in need. But today, we can see that our intention did NOT end up well in that part of the world. As of the writing of this book, we have major ongoing problems in the Middle East, and we have to put our best foot forward to try to stabilize the countries in that part of the globe. But we failed to recognize the people of some of these countries are not yet ready and were never exposed to liberties and freedoms. These populations have always succumbed to some strong man for guidance and strength. By doing what we think is best in these situations, we inadvertently created a vacuum in their system, and radical sections raised up in the now uncontrolled and unchecked environment left by our intervention. I can only repeat what my grandfather used to say, having lived in Tripoli most of his life. "A Shepherd knows his sheep." When you take the Shepherd out, some of the sheep become splintered and develop their own agenda and lose their way home.

Our country has seen our own evils, not to fully compare it to the above, but a somewhat more timid example is seen with the North versus South in our American Civil War. This internal war was responsible for much bloodshed and partisan alliances to some ideologies of those times. I am not an expert on our civil war, but the mutual understanding, compassion, freedom, and laws that create order ultimately brought our country together. From time to time, we need to adjust this understanding, using creativity and inclusionary referendums to keep our union and democracy the most liberal and free country in the world.

However, as I deviated from our story and our family experiences with the history of these parts of the world, we can learn from these facts above how to be inclusive with all of our fellow American citizens. In Libya, when the uprising and eventual coup of Qaddafi occurred, the Libyan monarchy came to an end. So did that tranquil country.

This is where my grandfather Vincenzo on my mother's side, introduced earlier, comes to play a role in the years after the war and all through the

1950s. Vincenzo worked on behalf of a prominent, influential Italian family that was given land during colonial times. He did not own the land but was a sharecropper. The newly established monarchy allowed the Italians to farm the land as long as a portion of the profits was used to benefit the monarchy. My grandfather cultivated and managed the production of olive oil, oranges, lemons, grapes, and wine, which he did all along, even before the war.

Grandfather Vincenzo on his cultivated land, 1937, during the Italian Colonial days.

My mother's family was living on what was described to me by my mother and her sisters as a large Napa Valley estate of the early 1950s in

Tripoli. My grandfather would make sure that his workers, the local Arabs, would get paid to produce the fruit of this land and deliver it to market. My mother, Rosa, recalls how her father would walk the many acres of fields on those sun-drenched, hot afternoons. The Arab workers would find relief from the heat under an olive or orange tree. My grandfather, walking the fields wearing the typical colonial grey clothes and boots, would sometimes find them napping instead of working. He would carry a container of fresh water with him and upon discovering a sleeping worker, he would release a portion of that water on them. This was a crude way to wake them up and a well-deserved reminder that he was paying them to work and not to sleep. That home, according to my mother, even today, was the most beautiful and accommodating house she had ever called home. She would narrate to me all about the home's seven large rooms and big basement, "cantina," in Italian terms. These rooms delivered comfort, and the large kitchen always had plenty of food harvested from my grandfather's fields. The cantina housed large barrels of wine and olive oil for the family and friends to last years. The local Arabs and the workers were also very friendly with my grandfather and his family. Unlike some bad colonialists of other countries, of which you may have read sad stories, my grandfather always took care of his workers. All he wanted was a good day's work for a fair day's pay.

She also recalls how during the Muslim holidays the workers would bring their celebratory foods to our house. Their main festive dish was called "Couscous" and it was made of whole-wheat semolina grain. This is not like what you buy today at the supermarket in a box. It was hand made from raw grain and mixed with a small amount of water to bind the small grains into larger ones. This was a tedious process done with the fingers, mostly by the local young women and wives, mixing this grain in a large circular pail, enough to feed the whole family and any invited guests. This whole wheat semolina grain was made to prepare the foundation of this fancy dish. All the relatives would reunite to enjoy this food during their religious and celebratory Muslim holidays. The couscous was slow cooked with steam vapor generated by a special cookware set. The bottom portion of the pan had water that boils on the stove and a matching top portion pan with small fine holes on the bottom would fit snugly on top of this water boiling unit. The semolina couscous was placed inside the top pan unit, where it cooked slowly with the water vapor. The couscous was turned from time to time as it slowly absorbed the steam and cooked. A light red sauce was prepared separately in a large deep skillet. The red sauce was prepared by mixing pre-seared lamb meat, chickpeas, potatoes, squash, carrots and many other vegetables until fully cooked. Traditional local Arab spices were added together to enhance the flavor of the couscous. This dish was a one-plate meal, each plate having the couscous on the bottom and the meat with the vegetables that were cooked in the red sauce all arranged on top of the grain.

When I describe this dish, my mouth starts to salivate and brings back memories of my mother, who, up to only ten years ago, was still preparing this dish for all of us. I must say that she enjoyed making it since it would bring back real nice memories from her days when she lived in Tripoli. It also brings fond memories, envisioning my father, now deceased, enjoying his humongous oversized deep special dish always placed first in front of him at dinner: a real treat for everyone throughout the years. This dish was also a motivation to bring back all of our family together at the same table. My mother described that this exact same ritual was carried out by the Arab families during her time in Tripoli. She would also remember how the Arab workers employed by my grandfather, would bring some of their Couscous dish to our house for our family to enjoy. This gesture reflected their appreciation and friendship for my grandfather and our family. This traditional dish, while a laborer's dish, played a large part through the decades to keep our family united, no matter what country we were living in.

After a brief courtship typical for those days between my mother Rosa and my father Giorgio, they married in 1954. The two families had the same

Italian origins, shared the same values and culture and it was almost a match made in heaven. My mother was seventeen years old and my father was twenty-three. You may wonder about my mother's young age but according to her, a seventeen-year-old girl then was much more mature than today's teenagers. Sorry Gen Z!

Shortly after the wedding, my father gave up his wild motorcycle racing, but remained working at the American base for a while longer. I was born about a year later. My two grandfathers were very happy that I was a boy - you know: those old Italians! It would have been just as fine if I had been a girl. As it was customary and respectful for the times, my name was given to me to honor my grandfather "Giuseppe." It was a great gift to both families to have a grandchild, which marked a new generation. The women in the families, especially my grandmother, Raffaella, Rosa's mother, were very pleased with my safe arrival.

Tripoli, 1955. Left to right: Aunt Maria, Raffaella holding me, Rosa, and Aunt Anna.

By the way, I am one of those babies that was born at home with the help of a midwife, again typical for the times. My mother also has two younger sisters; both of them are still alive, likewise for my mother. Even today, they always bring to my attention when we chat on the phone, the joy and warmth that I brought to the home being the first-born. It is also nice to know that since my mother's family home was so large, my parents initially decided to live in a portion of that house where they had privacy and my mother could get some help from her sisters during my early months. I guess my arrival and presence in the home was very joyous and I was treated like a living toy that arrived in the household. From what I hear, I was spoiled by everyone there. Everyone wanted to have his or her time with me every day, to hold me and share the care that a new baby needs. Giuseppe had a couple of homes that he owned nearby and he made one available to my father. My parents moved to one of these nearby homes after a few months. It was probably time to have my own room instead of sleeping in a crib in my parents' bedroom.

After the house relocation, my father also decided to stop working at the American base and opened a small car and truck repair shop with a close friend, Antonio. My father always nurtured all his friends, especially the ones from his youth, and kept in touch with them all the time no matter where he lived. Even if he was no longer working at the base, some of the American personnel there still asked my father to take them for weekend Safaris or desert trips. The extra money would come in real handy now, especially while his business was in its early days. These interactions with the Americans also allowed him to practice his English-speaking skills to keep it fresh in his mind. He always used to say you never know when lady luck knocks at your door: "You must be prepared at all times with all your skills in tip top shape."

Towards the end of the 1950s, there were rumors spreading around the city by the local Arab residents that brought some uneasiness to our young family. Every day, more subtle events were seen in the city, which fermented a somewhat uncomfortable atmosphere in Tripoli. Both of our families' elders sensed a different way of life was starting to take hold in that country. There was a nervousness in doing business in the city. It could not be seen but it was definitely there. There were rumors that tribal Arabs around the countryside did not like the current government, the monarchy of King Muhammad Idris Al-Sanusi. He was the head of state since the American's gave Libya independence after the War. King Idris had sided with Britain against the Germans during World War II. This made him an unpopular monarch. More and more Arabs were talking of inequalities in Libya under the King's government. Money was flowing to a few rich families rather than the average Arab. My grandparents sensed that eventually there would be an uprising and that all foreigners could be in danger. My father, now head of a family, was also very uneasy and started to investigate if the Italian government was offering any support to the Italian citizens that lived in Tripoli. He found out that the Italian government had already recognized this unsettling governmental situation in Libya for a while now.

It was a well-known fact that once Italy lost her three colonies Libya, Somalia, and Ethiopia after the war, the Italian government would eventually need to find a way to accommodate those Italian citizens that no longer wanted to live in those ex-colonies. Many of them could eventually decide to move back to Italy, even if many of them had deep roots since they lived in the ex-colony most of their adult lives. My father discovered through the Italian embassy in Tripoli that the Italian government was building new housing in Italy for these colonial citizens. Any of them that wanted to repatriate could apply and secure one of these new government-owned dwellings at a very low monthly rental premium. I believe what happened then was that a dialogue and discussion took place between all the family members. They all concluded that the good life in Tripoli was coming to an end soon. It was also known that if things got out of hand, it could be a very dangerous time where they could lose everything they owned and possibly their lives. Everyone decided that it was probably time to sell and get whatever they could before they lost it all. It must have been a devastating decision to leave that way of life behind and decide to move to a new home in Italy. These government dwellings were being built in several strategically placed cities around Italy. The only city that the Italian government was building these homes in that made sense for us was in the city of Messina, Sicily. The climate was not much different than the current one in which we lived. Sicily was also where my grandfather's roots came from while my grandmother was from the Naples area.

Everyone agreed that it was best for our families to leave Tripoli when the housing became available in Italy, since it was on a first come first served basis. The way I look at this situation is by reminding myself of the great quote: "*If life gives you lemons you make lemonade.*" To this day, my mother and all the currently living elders still cry thinking about that decision, but it had to be made. We were able to sell the houses and land for pennies on the dollar, because the Arab businessmen saw the opportunity and knew that we had no other choice. Change was coming fast to Libya. It would hit them soon just like a freight train. History would prove my father's and everyone else's decision to be the correct one. We did leave many years pre-maturely, but we were able to get some money for what we owned and bring back most of our belongings.

Muammar Qaddafi took over in the late sixties with a coup also known as the "al-Fateh Revolution" or the "September 1 Revolution," a military coup d'état in Libya carried out by the Free Officers Movement. This military group led by Colonel Muammar Qaddafi, led to the overthrow of

King Idris I. The Italians still there were told to leave immediately. Their properties were confiscated and they were allowed to take with them only two luggage bags each with personal belongings. In addition, almost all of the Italians buried in the cemeteries were also excavated and sent back to Italy on ships. The Revolution wanted no part of Italy or the past Italian colonialism. This was a disgrace and a slap in the face to the Italian government. History did not fare well for the Italians that remained in Libya during the coup. The Italian population virtually disappeared after the Libyan leader Muammar Qaddafi ordered the expulsion of most of the Italians (there were about 10,000) in 1970 left over. Only a few hundred of them were allowed to return to Libya in the 2000s. This incident is still being debated today and is a contentious point of order by the current elected Italian government. How did we allow this to happen without defending our Italian citizens caught up in the Qaddafi coup? I am sure the United States would have never allowed this shameful event to occur if it had impacted the Americans instead of the Italians.

Unfortunately, before my parents made the decision to leave Tripoli later on that year, my grandmother, Raffaella, fell ill. Nobody really knows what she suffered from, but it was speculated that it might have been pancreatic cancer. My grandfather brought her to Sicily for further testing and possible treatment. While in a hospital in Messina, the disease got the best of her and within a couple of months, she passed. This was a very tragic event for my grandfather and for all of us. She was a very caring and reserved woman that always stood by her husband, her one true love.

OUT OF ITALY

As you read this second part of the book, please keep in mind that the initial portion is written by gathering notes via the many interviews with my mother, her two sisters living in Italy, and with one of my father's work colleagues, still alive and living in Messina. I was way too young initially to recall and understand the events of the early days of our life in Messina. These notes shed light on those days and to the best of my knowledge are a true account of those early years in Messina following our departure from Libya.

This chapter brings into perspective why I titled this book *The Last Real Immigrant.* It will also enlighten our journey by recounting our life events, difficulties, and undertakings in our second home country. Among many things, you will read how my father, through many decades of his life, was able to accomplish and live a successful, vibrant life. I must say that he was much more successful at achieving this than I have been. I am not anywhere near his level, but I am working on it and will until the end. He did not walk on water, but some people could swear that he did. You will soon understand and envision the driving and daring force behind his character. You will also fully appreciate the real-life lessons that he has instilled in us, his kids, to make a difference whenever we can and give back to the country the fruits of our labor. Jesus states in the Bible, in Matthew 22:21 "Give to Caesar what belongs to Caesar, give to God what belongs to God." I said from the very start that this book is the history of our immigrant family, our life on three continents. I just recounted the first one in the initial portion of this book.

This second part is the platform that put us on the next path and propelled us to our next destination; it could have gone in a different direction but it went this way. We now are proud to say that all of us are living in the greatest and mightiest country on earth: AMERICA.

Our family always lived by those rules, obeyed the laws of the land and tried to live by example no matter which country we lived in. This is the family that was always looking for a better life and returning that opportunity, by giving back those fruits, with our skills and labor to the host country. We always wanted to show people and places, that we could work hard and earn our status, however small it was, in that society. My father was a firm believer that if you treat people fairly and honestly, they will treat you just the same. He was a person that always saw the glass half-full not half-empty. You may call him somewhat of a perfectionist. He would say, "If you do not have the time, do not do it. If you do not know how to do it, learn it first, try it first, and make sure it works. Only then, say, 'I can do it.'" He also said, "If people trust you with their resources, whatever they may be, make sure you return to them more than they invested in you." His optimistic view even during bad times brought a comfort and trust to everyone around him. His mind and body were always firing on all cylinders just like the engines that he worked with on a daily basis. As I recall him throughout the years, his ingenuity and logic were immeasurable. I, myself, also wonder today if he actually could walk on water. However, as we continue on our journey through the decades, you can be the judge of that.

So here we are, it is almost 1960. We have since left Tripoli and arrived in a city called Messina on the large island of Sicily. My father selected this location for several reasons. The main reason was that the Italian government had built a brand-new condominium complex of homes in Messina. This was the first site ready to host the re-settled Italian colonial families. These homes built by the Italian government were earmarked exclusively for the families that wanted to come back to the Italian homeland. My father was able to complete the application process while in Tripoli, via the local Italian embassy, and when his application was accepted he was notified and assigned one of these homes. His decision to relocate was not made lightly, as I mentioned earlier. When he and the other elders evaluated the current political situation in Libya together with the allocation of a new home in Italy by the government, the conclusion was logical. The city of Messina was part of our family's roots going back many decades. There is one other likely reason why my father selected Messina. The climate in Sicily closely resembled that of Tripoli. Finally, there was the fact that my grandmother, Raffaella, died in Messina. She was buried in the local cemetery. Relocating would give my grandfather some much needed consolation. Once my father found out that the apartments in Messina were ready to accept the new tenants, he put the whole family in motion to embrace this new chapter.

Once we arrived in Messina, we were suddenly confronted and challenged with many unpredicted realities. Even today, I always remind my kids that even if you think you have achieved greener pastures, always look back and make sure that you remember what you left behind. As the old Italian saying goes, "All that shines is not always gold." The first thing that was evident upon arrival and strikingly sobering was that our large seven room home in Tripoli had suddenly shrunk to a relatively small two-bedroom condominium. It was a first-floor unit in a large condominium complex very close to the center of town. The home, as I mentioned, was brand new, recently built but no larger than 1,000 square feet. It had one bathroom, a large dining/kitchen area, and a short corridor with access to two bedrooms. I can say with much genuineness that our condo, compared to the older ones built around us, was much more comfortable. Many of those older units lacked up to date facilities that we took for granted. But don't think for a moment that we could splurge in any way or form. All of the money was well accounted for and made to stretch as much as possible.

The condominium complex had a total of five floors. Our apartment also had a small open-faced veranda off the kitchen that looked at the city street; it was no bigger than nine feet by six feet. In fact, this became my favorite place where I spent a lot of my time as a young boy. Here, I would find some refuge, and a place to call my own. This veranda also hosted a large tub to hand wash the laundry. Let us not forget, that the very first residential washing machines had made their first public appearance around this time. They were very expensive and only a handful of people could afford them, notwithstanding the installation of the plumbing infrastructure. None of the apartments came equipped with a washing machine.

The structure was built entirely of cement with reinforced steel on its exterior walls. This type of construction was mandated and still remains the construction code today in the city of Messina. The reason for this high strength building construction is that a great earthquake almost completely destroyed the city of Messina in 1908. The earthquake was of 7.1 magnitude on the Richter scale. Its epicenter occurred in the Strait of Messina, a body of water that separates the busy port city of Messina in Sicily and Reggio Calabria across on the Italian mainland. Its precise epicenter was pinpointed to the northern Ionian Sea area close to the narrowest section of the Strait, the location of Messina. This quake almost completely leveled the city of Messina and according to records, 75,000 people were killed in the city and surrounding suburbs. On the other side of the strait in the city of Reggio Calabria, some 25,000 more people lost their lives. The following tsunami about ten minutes after the earthquake caused more devastation and deaths. Messina lost almost 50% of its population and most of the city infrastructure and buildings crumbled to the ground. If you happen to visit the island of Sicily and look at the many cities on this island, you will definitely notice a difference when you visit the city of Messina. The city is relatively new when you compare her to the other major cities in Sicily that have been there for centuries. The earthquake destroyed much of the historical center, so there is very little left from pre-1908. Most of the downtown buildings are less than 100 years old. These are considered very new by Italian standards as much of Italy's historical structures date back thousands of years. To minimize the danger of future earthquakes and more destruction, this rigid building code was established and put in effect to help minimize the damage of any future earthquakes. A footnote here: I was there for several less minor earthquakes during the 1960s. These happened when I was a child. However, even at that young age I can tell you that the feeling you have during one of these events is surreal. You feel powerless and utterly small, completely controlled by an immense force larger than life. You get to realize and reflect upon just how fragile humans are on this planet; any large cataclysmic event can put an end to our life on earth in seconds.

Our new home was not what my mother would have imagined, but given the low rent payment to the government and the brand-new construction, we could have ended up in a worse place. We did not have much of a choice but to leave the African continent and plant our feet on safer ground. After all we are Italians, and this was our original homeland for better or for worse. At least for the time being, we had a roof over our heads and a new place to call home. Once we settled into our new home, my father had important matters to address. It was his duty to provide financial means and a respected way of life in this new city that adopted us. The first point of order for my father was that he had to find employment as soon as possible. The other pressing issue which compounded that need was that my mother was expecting the fourth member of our family, my soon to be sister. My grandfather, Vincenzo, asked my father to take his two younger daughters, my mother's younger sisters Maria, aged nineteen and Anna, aged seventeen, to Messina. He remained in Tripoli for a little while longer to sell the few assets that we left behind. As you can imagine, the apartment became even smaller when everyone was there. I slept on a pull-out bed in the living room. Once my sister was born, she would be sleeping in a crib in my parents' bedroom. Maria and Anna slept together in the other bedroom.

My grandfather, when he finally arrived in Messina almost a year later, was in his late-sixties. I can definitely say this for my grandfather's arrival in Sicily: it was known as the lowest point of his life. From then on, everything went downhill for him, as my mother explained to me. I can faintly remember people and places during these early days in Messina, as I was only four years old. I am very sad when I think about my grandfather during that time. He had reached his retirement years, lost his wife two years earlier, and should have been able to live what we today call his golden years in Tripoli where he grew up. He had worked hard his entire life and had everything there that he and his family needed. He lived the life that few people lived, but he and his family had to leave it all behind in what seemed a heartbreaking decision and that was exactly what happened to him. I wonder how I would feel if I were in his shoes: finding myself, all of a sudden, enclosed in a small apartment in a city that is foreign to you. It brings tears to my eyes just thinking about it. If I was old enough to remember those ugly details of what really happened then, it would affect me even more. What a personal human tragedy that must have been! You do not wish this kind of event on your worst enemy, yet it happened to my grandfather.

Meanwhile, my other grandfather Giuseppe was looking to do the same thing, but he remained in Tripoli for a little longer. He had many more things to take care of since he owned several homes that were rented to Arab families. He was in a slightly better financial situation than Vincenzo, but he would also experience his own shocking reality once he moved to Messina.

He asked my father to find him a suitable home to buy that would be ready for him once he was to able leave Tripoli.

As I mentioned earlier, Messina is a seaport city separated by the Strait of Messina from the mainland of Italy. This strait measures less than two miles at its narrowest point but it is more than three miles from the Port of Messina. The channel at its deepest point is over 800 feet deep. The waters are not for the faint hearted to navigate. There are very strong currents that crisscross throughout the strait. The reason for these currents is that two seas meet at this point. The Tyrrhenian Sea to the north and the Ionian Sea to the south.

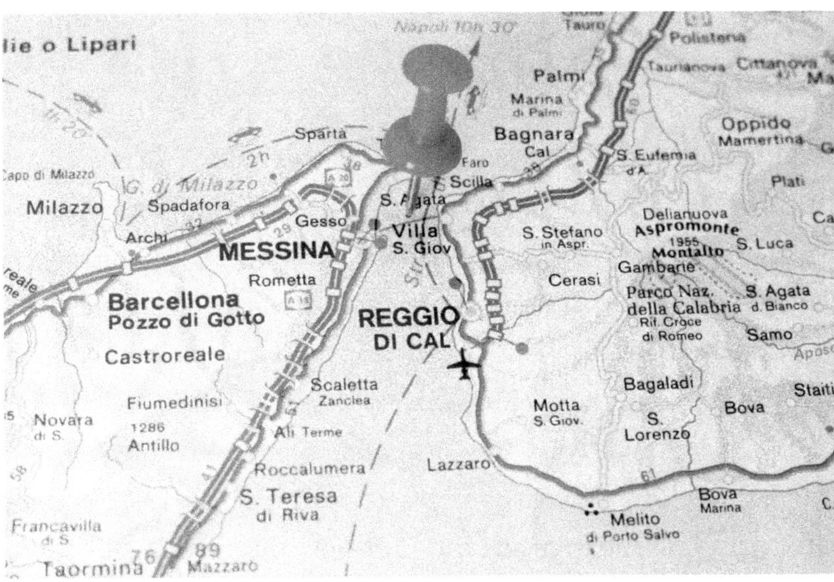

Strait of Messina.

As you can picture, the only way to cross to the mainland and vice versa is by boat. This trip takes almost one hour but most of those commercial ships are also capable to carry both cars and trucks. Other larger ships owned by the Italian government allow the country's train system to be loaded on board to continue the journey to the Italian mainland; obviously, the reverse is also true. The trains are broken apart in smaller sections, put on short rail systems on the boats, and then reconnected on the other side. You can stay on the train during this trip or you can disembark, have a cup of coffee or a snack at the ship café and are free to walk about the ship. It is an incredible experience to travel across the Strait of Messina with either a car or a train. When I was older, I was taken across many times as a four-hour getaway by my parents. It was a fun trip and the fare was very affordable. It was quite an experience just to lean on the rails and enjoy the view from the water. The sights are spectacular. I strongly recommended it if you find yourself travelling through Southern Italy. There are some cool videos documenting this experience on YouTube that are worth viewing.

Before our arrival in Messina, there was a company called "Rodriquez Cantieri Navali" located within the port infrastructure of the city. The translation is "Rodriquez Naval Shipyard." This was a large shipyard started in the early 1900s by Messina's prestigious Rodriguez family. They were considered to be the unofficial royalty of the city. In their early days, the shipyard provided repair facilities for ships and during the war for military equipment for the Italian Navy. The owner and naval engineer, Carlo Rodriquez, was a thinker, an innovator, and a visionary. He spent a lot of time traveling abroad and meeting different pioneers and entrepreneurs of those times. He had seen a conception of and the testing of earlier prototypes of a small vessel called the hydrofoil during and shortly after the war in Germany. The hydrofoil usually consists of a wing-like structure mounted on struts below the hull, or across the keels in this variety of boats. As a hydrofoil-equipped watercraft increases its speed, the hydrofoil elements below the hull(s) develops enough lift to raise the hull out of the water, which obviously greatly reduces hull drag. It is a perfect solution to transport people at high speed across seas, large rivers, and lakes. In 1956, this shipyard in Messina built the first hydrofoil that was capable of carrying up to seventy-two people at a speed of thirty-five knots, which translates to approximately forty miles per hour. This meant that you could go across the Strait of Messina in twenty minutes. You can bring your luggage and personal bags right onboard and then continue to your final destination on the land side of Italy by other means of transportation.

The first hydrofoils to provide high-speed public transportation between Messina and Reggio Calabria.

The Rodriquez Cantieri was always scouting for specialized and skilled personnel with talent, to help in the construction of these new hydrofoils. My father saw that opportunity and applied for a position as an experienced engine mechanic at the Rodriquez Cantieri. His previous knowledge with truck engines and other heavy diesel equipment matched very well with the needs of the mechanical position in the shipyard. The engines were an integral part of these ships and the company was always on the lookout for individuals experienced in diesel engine systems. Within a few weeks, my father was hired and began working at the Rodriquez shipyard in the engine assembly and maintenance sector for the hydrofoils. The pay was not the best, but it was above the average blue collar worker's salary at the time. It provided our family a comfortable life in Italy, thanks to his incredible ingenuity and work ethic. This was the beginning of a great job and eventually a great and important relationship that begins when you least expect it.

My mother gave birth that year to a baby girl. She was named Alba, and to this day, I am not sure why she received that name. It may have been because she was born in the early morning hours. The name "Alba" means "Sunrise" in the Italian language. In any case, she was a much-needed addition to the household. There was already a boy, me, and now a girl. Today, I joke about that since I also have a daughter and a son. I tell them and others that they are our life replacements when their mother and I pass on. People say I am somewhat ironic in saying that, but it is one way of looking at the tree of life.

My new sister gave the home some needed enjoyment during those early times while we adjusted to our new life. The new surroundings and, frankly, the City of Messina as a whole was, for all of us, somewhat of a challenge. For my part, I started school attending first grade at a Catholic school, conveniently located just across the street from our condominium complex. The location of this school gave my mother a breath of relief, because she just walked me across the street, dropped me off at the school, and would be back home within ten minutes.

My mother's day was also challenging. She attended to the new baby and also to her aging father. Fortunately, my Aunt Anna provided a helping hand in the household. My Aunt Maria, now twenty-years-old, was offered a working opportunity in a clothing factory in northern Italy shortly after we arrived. She decided to leave Messina and began her independent life in northern Italy. This happened after her father, Vincenzo, arrived in Messina in early 1960.

While my father was working at the shipyard, my mother would take care of the household, attending to the family's day-to-day needs. Our new condominium, since it was exclusively built for the Italian ex-colonialists, was called in Italian 'Case per I profughi D'Africa." The closest translation is "Homes for repatriated citizens from the African Italian colonies." The condominium complex housed over 100 units divided into two large five story buildings. There was a large, mostly cemented, courtyard separating these buildings that was used as a playground. This area also contained some bare land plots, around the edges on the backside of each home. The first-floor tenants usually were assigned the usage of this small parcel of land. If we did not want to take care of it, we could offer it to any of the neighbors residing on the upper floors to use. That meant that we had a little piece of land where we could plant flowers or vegetables. My mother was too busy managing the household to do any of that. She asked her father if he wanted to use this little garden and take care of it. It would keep him busy and also allow him to spend time outside breathing some fresh air.

My grandfather as you recall in the "Out of Africa" part of this book, used to cultivate acres and acres of land in Tripoli. He had more than fifty Arab employees working the land. This small parcel of land, maybe measuring about sixty feet by twelve feet, was a little speck of land compared to what he had just a couple of years before. My mother probably thought that it would give him the opportunity to forget about the past, but I think it backfired because it actually reminded him of what he once had and what he had lost. I believe that this probably depressed him even more and reminded him of his land in Tripoli. He never actually stepped foot on that parcel of dirt. He also felt like a stranger in this new city. It may have been his homeland, but one that he never lived in. This must have contributed to his declining health. Shortly thereafter, he was diagnosed with having a heart condition with some loss of his mental faculties.

Our condominium complex was surrounded on all sides by a five-foot-tall perimeter wall. The wall had a lovely styled two-foot open steel rail on top of it. An adult could easily scale it, so it really did not serve as a security barrier, but it was an additional definition to identify the borders of the condominium complex. There were two large, tall steel gates along the wall located at two strategic entry and exit points. These gates provided access to the playground and the land parcels that I mentioned earlier. All of the homes had visibility to most of these grounds from their backside windows or balconies. Unfortunately, my mother did not allow me to play in this recreational space until I was much older. She was very protective in sending me there alone without supervision and she did not have the time to bring me there because my baby sister kept her busy. I really missed the opportunity to go play in our playground during those times. I think this brings into perspective why I liked our small veranda; it was my own private open space to the outside world. The veranda entrance was located right off the kitchen and living room. I found some peace and serenity in that space to enrich myself by reading books and magazines such as Superman or Batman, all in the Italian language, of course.

My father Giorgio would leave the house everyday around 7:00 AM and would not come back home until 6:00 PM or later. His new job required him to work overtime hours since the shipyard was also projecting for the second generation of the hydrofoil. This was a much larger version of the hydrofoil model. Our family could use the extra money from his overtime, and it also showed the Rodriguez Cantieri that he was a dedicated member of the team. My father was a loyal employee on top of his wonderful and unique mechanical skills. He was the newcomer there and wanted to stand apart with his honest and fair work ethics.

In Messina and throughout Italy's smaller cities, there were not many cars in circulation in the early 1960s. Vespa's, motorbikes, and bicycles were the main mode of private transportation, particularly in the southern portion of Italy. My father, however, was able to purchase a car by the end of his first year at the shipyard. We became the proud owners of a 1960 Fiat 500. You may be familiar with this car since Fiat Chrysler America introduced this model in 2016 to the American market. The bodylines of the American-built Fiat 500 were very similar to our original Fiat 500. My family and a few others were one of a handful of people that owned a car in our complex during those years. I believe that the money used to buy this car was made possible by my father's overtime pay. You could say that we were somewhat privileged to be able to get around the city with such ease. We were also one of the few families that had the luxury of taking weekend trips to the nearby beaches or the mountainside because of it. Our family really enjoyed exploring the suburbs of the city and meeting new people during those early years in Italy.

The most difficult aspect of our early years was that we felt like outsiders in our new city and even in our complex. Starting a new life where you do not know anybody can be a very abysmal feeling. The language was not a factor but meeting new people and interacting with them was a bit intimidating, at least initially. To bring life to the forefront in those years, there were no supermarkets then. If you needed to buy common foods like canned goods or cold cuts, you would go to a local general food store. If you desired meat, you would go to a butcher shop. If you wished to buy some fish for dinner, you would go to the fish market. Each day, the local fishermen would sell their daily catch right by the sea wall sidewalk. To buy bread, you went to a bakery. Wine, beer, and other alcohol was sold in a specialty store. You may think that the food was more wholesome and fresher then, and you are probably right. When you entered each of these stores you could see and smell many of the items that were prepared or delivered daily. When you shopped you also had the opportunity to engage with the staff, and most of the time it was the store owner. In Italy, we called them "botteghe" or "family-owned small food shops." My mother would visit them at least twice a week. There was also the experience of interacting with the other customers who were waiting their turn to be serviced.

One interesting fact about our family was that since all of us grew up in Tripoli, we spoke only the proper Italian language. In Messina, many of the locals spoke the Sicilian dialect. Only the aristocrats and people that attended a higher level of education spoke the real Italian language. These educated people also spoke the local dialect, but preferred the native Italian to converse. They would switch their language to the dialect only if they needed to identify themselves as a native Sicilian. In our case, many people would identify us as non-Sicilian because we did not speak the dialect and we did not carry any other accent. We were asked on many occasions where we came from. Sometimes it would be a great conversation, but sometimes the other person did not even know about Tripoli and Libya or where they were located.

As the first couple of years went by, our family became somewhat integrated in our condominium complex. When we migrated to Messina, we were one of the first initial families that moved into the building. By 1962, a very diverse population occupied the apartments. They all came from the Northern part of Africa. Some lived in other older Italian colonies like Ethiopia and Somalia. Regardless of where they came from, everyone had their own story just like ours. Each family for one reason or another had to leave their previous home and were forced to establish new lives in a new place.

By 1963, I was in fourth grade at the same Catholic school next to our building. As we all know, Italy is considered a majority Catholic country. The Pope lives in Vatican City, an independent state located within the boundary of the city of Rome. Throughout the centuries, the Catholic Church played a large role in the life and customs of most of the Italian people. My family is Catholic and the elementary school next to our condominium was part of the local parish church, located next to the school building. I believe it was called "Sacred Heart Catholic Church." It was understood, even if not enforced, that all the families that had children at the elementary school were expected to attend most of the solemn services, including Sunday Mass.

My homeroom teacher, a nun, asked me during the fourth grade if I would like to be an altar boy for the weekly mass. I guess I always stood out, which somewhat has been my story for most of my life, but it really started during those early years. My character evolved very eloquently during my childhood. My parents were very strict and they expected respect and obedience in our home. I believe that the teacher, knowing our family's background and origins, saw in me some qualities different than that of the local population. My teacher sent a note home to my parents in order to get their approval to be an altar boy. Obviously, it was only a formality, since their acceptance was expected from God-fearing parents! When the church makes a request, you need to accept or suffer the consequences.

My father was not much of a churchgoer and did not qualify as a God-fearing parent. My mother really played both roles here, with my father's blessing. I do not want to sound hypocritical, even if it may sound so, but a married woman's role during this period, especially in Italy, was to give credit to the husband and to carry on the family tradition. Even if my father did see the note, it was up to my mother to carry out those additional tasks. In our case, my father worked a lot and when Sunday came, he just wanted to rest and spend quality time at home or take the family on a relaxing afternoon car trip after we attended church. Remember that there were no weekends then. Most people worked Monday through Saturday. Some of them would work half a day on Saturday, if they were given the option. The only people that worked five days a week were government workers.

As long as my mother would show up at most Sunday Masses, especially when I was one of the altar boys, things were fine. Many times, she would ask my Aunt Anna to accompany her. In addition, if my baby sister Alba was on her best behavior and was not too cranky, she would also attend Sunday Mass. From time to time, maybe every few months, my mother would try to drag my father to church. She would tell him "Giorgio, if you do not show in person once in a while to church, what would people think! Maybe that we are not practicing Catholics. I do not want to always use the same excuse when the other parents, parishioners ask about you and tell them that you worked overtime last night. It just does not look good." So, perhaps several times a year, my father would get dressed up and accompany my mother to Sunday Mass.

One thing about my father was that he always observed the sacred holidays, which I recall quite well. The solemn holidays still remind me of some significant events. It may shed some light about my character, especially during those very young years of my childhood days in Italy. The following accounts may be considered unrealistic from an eight-year-old child's perspective, but they are, in fact, true.

When I was almost eight years old, I possessed a memory that could challenge most of today's most eloquent orators. I was a sharp reader, spoke quite well for my age, and could remember entire paragraphs just by reading them a few times. I must have had a photographic memory. The text remained in my mind for days, everything to the letter, including the commas. During the Christmas and Easter holiday season, it was customary for my elementary school parish to fervently celebrate those holidays. This religious custom was spear-headed by the nuns, who were also the teachers at the school. They worked closely with the two parish priests to carry out these traditions every year. The parish was always proud to introduce some of their talented students that exceled in creativity to the parishioners, especially during Sunday services. I believe that this was all coordinated to enhance the Catholic educational system in order to distance themselves from the public-school sector. Some of the higher-ranking nuns, together with the participation of the parish priests, would write a two-to-three-page oration to celebrate the birth of Jesus at Christmas and the Resurrection at Easter. These sermons would take place at the parish church during the midnight mass on Christmas Eve and at the noon mass on Easter Sunday.

A photo of me engaged during a dress rehearsal of my oration.

Somehow, and I can't remember how this happened, I was selected to deliver these addresses to all of the worshippers that attended these sacred masses. I am going to describe only one of these events, since I was selected again in fifth grade. The initial one is really the only one that matters, and I could stamp it as my greatest personal accomplishment to this day. I can still remember that first time like it was yesterday. The others were less impactful because I had normalized reciting these orations. At a young age, I was led to believe that it was my vocation or my duty to the Catholic Church and our religion.

Our parish church was quite large, just like many of the churches in Italy are. It could easily accommodate 400 seated parishioners, plus additional overflow around the back and the inside perimeter after all the seats were occupied. This made this church even more intimidating because there were people everywhere during these two major holidays.

The memorization started about one month before the two holidays with many rehearsals also taking place in the classroom. The narration of this manuscript was a pretty sophisticated account of verses from the Bible that celebrated Christmas and Easter. The Catholic Church then followed the old Latin traditions for all of the Christian holidays. The script was part of the Mass celebration and was delivered and eulogized by poor me, during the Holy ceremony. I would practice and eventually memorize to the letter the complete written script. This became my after-school work for several weeks. My parents were made aware of this extracurricular activity and, as you can imagine, my mother was most proud that I was chosen for this task. It was a grueling job, especially for my young age. In the following weeks, other nuns would drop in to see my progress and also help me to fine-tune my tone and oral delivery of this speech. The last week before the Holiday Mass, I would practice my now memorized eulogy every afternoon in the main church standing at the actual podium on the altar. This usually took place around 4:00 PM or 5:00 PM when the church would be mostly empty. I would step up to the podium and turn the microphone on and begin practicing the delivery. The nun would sit in the front pew looking directly at me with her written copy in hand and I with the memorized version in my head. I would start this task and she would follow me letter by letter gesturing when to pause, and when to lower or raise my voice. This was not easy work for an eight-year-old child. The words were not easy. Some of them were in Latin but the nun would explain their meaning, so that I could affirm them and enunciate them better.

Even now, thinking back to that time, how did I do it? It seems to me that when you are very young, you are fearless and your defenses are not fully developed. This allows an innocent level of recognition and a courageous way to attack duties and tasks. By delivering this assignment successfully, the Christmas and Easter holidays now have a magical meaning for me, which I carry with me for the rest of my life. The delivery of this celebratory oration for the Christmas holiday was to take place during midnight mass on Christmas Eve, but it actually started at 11:00 PM. This particular liturgy is very elaborate and prolonged since it celebrates the birth of Jesus Christ. That said, could you imagine me at that young age? It was past midnight and I had to deliver such a stressful performance.

The church was filled to capacity and many people were standing in the overflow areas in the back and on the sides. The scent of incense was everywhere! This aroma blended with that of the many flowers and poinsettia plants placed all around the large altar floor. The organ would play and the choir would sing from the back elevated floor of the church. Many of the people joined in these songs from the church main floor. The sounds, the church vastness, and the aromas still play with my senses. It impacts me even today during the Christmas holiday season.

As the Holy Mass started, I would find a seat on a chair at the side of the altar, awaiting my destiny with a pounding heart and sweaty palms. Then, all of the sudden, my time arrives. After the first gospel, which is never ending during the midnight mass, the priest would end it by saying "The Lord be with you." The congregation would answer "And also with you." As a side note for the avid readers who would like more details, the whole mass in those days was mostly in Latin, something that probably only a few of us recall. The priest would proceed and say "Now we have a special Christmas celebratory oration that rejoices us tonight in celebrating the birth of our Jesus Christ, the Savior of the world. One of our talented students at our elementary school will deliver this celebratory address." My name was not mentioned to the audience, which was okay with me. I knew a few of my neighbors attending, but the majority were complete strangers.

As I approached the podium, the nun that had been working with me over the last month or more would take her place in a reserved front seat directly facing me. She would be there to give me, what I hoped, was the support and a soft suggestion should my memory lapse. There was a complete silence as I moved toward the podium and escalated the few steps that lead to the platform. I recall the screeching of one of the steps that lead to the top platform. This reminded me of those horror movies that my parents did not want me to watch on late night TV or in the movie theaters. You know the ones when the camera shows a frightened woman approaching the top of the dark stairs, giving away her presence to the enemy.

Once I arrived at the top, I had an overarching view of all the people gathered in the church. I could see all the way to the back. I tapped the microphone softly with one of my tiny fingers to make sure it was on. The tapping sound greatly amplified by the microphone rebounded throughout the whole church, bringing chills up and down my young spine. Instantly, the nun gave me a queue to start speaking. My voice resounded strongly, slightly squeaky, but pleasantly within the great walls and tall ceiling of the church, almost astounding myself. I realized that this was very different from what I was used to during the practice sessions.

The church was now full of people instead of being empty during my rehearsals. After the initial few sentences, I suddenly felt no fear. I was no longer afraid, and I became stronger and in charge of this liturgy from my perch on the altar. Everyone was paying close attention to every one of my words that I was enunciating. They were not simple words or sentences. After all, the priest and the nuns had put a little bit of sweat into it. I stopped briefly at the commas and longer at the periods. The nun in front of me would conduct my speech just like a conductor at a symphony, or much like one of the speech prompters used today by politicians. I recall that it probably lasted at least ten minutes to cover all three single spaced pages recollected and spoken from my memory.

I look at this today, like I said, as my lifetime Catholic contribution to the night before Christmas. I deserve to go to heaven just for that! I definitely could not do that today, and would stumble even if I was asked just to read it. As I look at that day and the other occasions that followed, I wonder if it was actually me or maybe I had some kind of alien living in my body. I get reminded today of that 1996 John Travolta movie "Phenomenon," obviously on a much smaller scale, which I highly encourage everyone to see. The movie is about becoming a supernatural talented being for a short time when a bright alien light hits John Travolta, the main actor in this movie. I did not miss a word during that speech delivery. I still remember how I visualized the contents of the pages in my mind. It was as if I was reading the pages imprinted in my head.

When I finished, the parishioners applauded my delivery. I gracefully descended from the podium and placed myself back on my chair until the mass ended. I recall that after the conclusion of the liturgy, as people were leaving via the back of the church, some of the attendees in the first few rows came up to me as I was descending the altar. They included many of the leading nuns that made it all possible. Many of them hugged me as if I were their child protégé. I would feel their thick cotton black and white robes overtaking my entire body as they embraced me and told me "Well done, Joseph!" My mother would also find her way to the front with a proud looking aura in her beautiful, tailored dress. The nuns would congratulate her for my outstanding performance, which she absorbed to the fullest.

To this day, I cannot recall if my father attended any of these events in fourth and fifth grade. I know that he was not in the front of the church, but I am sure that he was probably in the back of the church keeping his usual low church profile. I recall a total of four of these events in my last two years at that school. Like I said, my father's role was to be the man of the house. He was not too fond of the church's strict laws and of attending weekly services. Maybe he was somewhat incredulous. This part of my education was best left to be handled by my mother. He just wanted it to be right, that I grew up respecting the church, and all the adults that were part of my upbringing and life. Giorgio was fine just to be the father and breadwinner figure.

That following year in March, my mother gave birth to her third child and the last member of our household. This was a baby boy and he was named Vincenzo, in honor of her father. My grandfather was still living in our home when my brother was born, but he was not doing well. I guess the solitude of those days, the sadness of his two losses - his wife and his land - affected his physical health. He was seeing doctors often and the medications were probably contributing to his poor mental health.

I do not recall much about my brother's birth, even if I was seven years old. It remains a foggy experience for me. I recall that a strange woman came to the house on that day. She was carrying a large black handbag and went directly to see my mother in the bedroom; it must have been the midwife. I do recall that Aunt Anna took me out to the nearby seafront walkway and she bought me ice cream as we walked the palm-tree lined waterfront of Messina. When we returned home, I saw a new baby that was crying wrapped in a white blanket, placed in a small crib in my mother's bedroom. My father was not there from my recollection. He was probably working overtime on that day or could have been out of town. There were very few phones in those days and we did not have one. I guess the family was now complete.

During that same year, Aunt Anna met a nice, well-educated man. He was the only child of a prominent family in Messina with a long Italian history that went back through the centuries, and also with some royalty titles associated with them. During his courtship of my aunt, he used to come over to our house often since she was living with us. His name was Franco and he was well-spoken but somewhat shy. However, with me, the oldest child, he was very engaging. My grandfather stayed very quiet when Franco used to visit his daughter. I think my grandfather was showing signs of not being fully mentally engaged, which made things a little bit awkward for everyone. In the Italian culture, even today, we expect the man of the household to be responsible of all the family members' wellbeing. Given the fact that my grandfather was losing some of his faculties, my father was left to play that role. My father looked after my mother's sister, Anna, when possible, to make sure that she was dating a nice man and things were progressing well. I think Franco understood our forced immigration from Tripoli and our family history. As I recall, he was an educated scholar that attended the University of Messina. His father was a well-connected gentleman working for the Italian government in the civil navy sector. Since his son was brought up with high expectations and in a conservative fashion, my parents took notice of his well-spoken personality and proficiency of the Italian language. I vividly remember an event that took place on January 6th.

The occasion was the Feast of the Epiphany, which is celebrated on January 6th. Epiphany commemorates the 12th day of Christmas when the three Wise Men arrived at the manger bearing gifts for the baby Jesus. It is a national holiday in Italy when most people don't work, and the tradition is called La Befana. The traditional Christmas holiday season in Italy lasts through the Epiphany festivity. La Befana has been an Italian tradition since the thirteenth century, and it comes from a Christian legend rather than from pop culture. According to the Italian legend, La Befana, a witch-like woman airborne herself by riding on a broom. She refused to join the Wise Men on their journey to see the baby Jesus. When she regrets her decision, she sets out to bring gifts to the Child but never finds him. Instead, she leaves gifts for other children. Italian children leave out their long socks at their bedside and put a stocking next to them for the Befana to fill on the night of January 5th, Epiphany Eve. I grew up with this tradition and when I was young, every Epiphany Eve, I would leave a stocking provided by my mother hung at the end of my bed post. According to tradition, if you were good that year you would receive gifts and candy but if you fell short on your behavior, La Befana would leave you lumps of coal. I never received coal even if I should have in some of those years. My parents played the Befana and when my siblings and I were sleeping, they would sneak in my bedroom and put gifts that they purchased for us kids in the stockings left at each bedside. The next day it would be just like Christmas Day in America. Hopefully you would find nice gifts when you woke up in the morning. This day along with all of the other days of Christmas are celebrated with a traditional Italian sweet cake. Most common is the Panettone, a bread-like loaf that is one of my favorites. It is now a popular American dessert, enjoyed as a sweet festive addition during the Christmas season. It is found in many food stores here in America.

Franco came to visit our home often since he and Anna were now engaged. On that day, he came over to the house and brought Anna a nice gift and flowers. I do not recall Anna's gift, but I do recall that he also brought me a gift. It was a highly sophisticated toy police kit, a much more elaborate version than the ones that you would find today at Wal-Mart or Target. This kit came in a large box and contained all kinds of the very items that a police officer or a detective would possess. While there were no firearms, it contained liquid to pick up fingerprints, just like the real thing! It did have toy handcuffs, badges, and a child-sized police hat. I believe the kit was designed to stimulate a child's understanding of what it takes to be in the world of law enforcement. It was very unusual and probably not readily available; I wonder where he found it. Epiphany 1963 and this particular gift, though it is long since gone, is something that I will forever hold dear in my heart. The holiday itself was always a coveted time for me during my childhood years in Italy. There are many memories of Epiphany that are forever rooted in me which I really cherish.

Another of my most wonderful childhood Epiphany memories was brought to me by my father's employer, which celebrated that holiday every year for all of their employees' youngsters. The Rodriguez shipyard gave all the employees' children a delightfully unforgettable celebration. Not many companies were able to do that. I am not sure when or how that tradition started, but it certainly was an enjoyable time for all of the children. I was a lucky and eager beneficiary for all the years that my father worked at the shipyard. The company compiled a list of all their employees' kids including their gender and age. I am not sure how that was done, perhaps from a questionnaire that was circulated to all their employees. Someone well connected with the company would be given the task during the month of December to go out and buy toys for all of the children.

On Epiphany, the shipyard was closed but it would turn itself into a Santa Claus Village. They would clear the large metal working tables in one of their manufacturing hangers and move them together. These tables would be filled with hundreds of strong, white paper bags each containing gifts. Some of them were quite large. Each bag was closed, stapled, and labelled with the employee's name and his child's name. I recall that almost all of the workers would attend this festive gathering. They would bring all of their children if they were old enough to attend. After a brief ceremony by members of the management and some refreshments, the name calling started. Each employee would approach the large table and collect a bag or bags - one for each child in their family. I eagerly remember the anticipation of receiving and opening my large bag or just to peek and see what the company bought for me. This was a very unique way to reward the employees and their children, and it made everyone feel proud that they were an integral part of the Rodriquez family enterprise. It also gave the opportunity for everyone to meet each other's kids which established what we now call collaboration via their youngsters. I believe it benefitted the company by building a strong team spirit at the shipyard. The toys were quite elaborate by those days' standards. I also believe that they spent somewhat more for the children of some key employees. My toys were rather sophisticated and expensive, probably not something that my parents could or would even consider buying for me. Most of the toys were state of the art electronic mechanical toys with lights and moving parts. They also came with batteries included so that my parents did not have to go out and spend additional money. I recall many nice toys during those years like a large moving Army tank with lights and sound that would automatically redirect itself if it would come in contact with an obstruction. There was also an American Air Force fighter jet complete with wired remote control that was loaded with lights and made real jet sounds. A large, light up gun with laser and sound features was another incredibly generous gift that was offered. What a delightful event this was for all the children, and what a great company it was for my father to work for.

Shortly after the holidays, Aunt Anna married Franco. I remember that event; not all the details that I would have liked, but enough to recall some of the memories and expand on it. I was just about nine years old then, but very aware of our family gatherings. This wedding was one of those high points.

By 1964 standards, this wedding was more than you would expect in a city like Messina and especially in relation to the neighborhood in which we lived. Since my new Uncle Franco came from a notable family with substantial assets, the affair was pretty much the talk of the condominium complex when it happened. The site of a large white limousine parked in front of our condominium entrance to pick up the bride and us for the wedding was not a common event in that part of the city. I recall that many people living in the other apartments were out on the sidewalk or out on their balcony to watch us getting into this limousine. There were no bridesmaids; my mother was the matron of honor. My grandfather was not in good physical condition but, with the help of my father, was also able to attend. Once we arrived at the church, he was able to slowly walk my aunt down the aisle with his cane to make the traditional ceremonial walk with his daughter to wed her husband. My brother was the only one missing that day since he was still a baby. My mother left him with our good friends, the neighbors that lived next door to our home. We were all dressed with newly purchased clothes. My sister Alba was almost five and was chosen to be the ring bearer. After the church ceremony, we drove to a beautiful location by the sea. It was a classy high-end restaurant that Franco's parents arranged and paid for. The guests in attendance were mostly on the groom's side since we were such a small family with no extended family nearby. I believe a couple of close family friends were also invited. It was a very joyous time for everyone and our newly-acquired family. I am sure that my father was also quite pleased that my mother's sister found a nice man and would move to a newly purchased condominium nearby to start their new life together. The now married couple left for a wedding trip to Greece and the islands on an ocean liner for about ten days following the wedding. This was somewhat of an uncommon occurrence in Southern Italy since the economy was not firing on all cylinders during those times.

When Franco and Anna came back, they moved into their new two-bedroom home about a mile from our home. Notwithstanding their needs to spend time together as a young couple, Anna recognized that her father, Vincenzo, could not be taken care of by my mother anymore. She was alone all day and now had three kids. After a couple of months, Anna decided to bring her father to live with them in their new home. Their apartment, having two bedrooms, could accommodate my grandfather even if he needed attention during the day. My aging grandfather would enjoy a more relaxed life since my siblings and I were young and would be loud and run around our apartment just like any kid our age would. My father appreciated this action from his sister in-law. It made good sense and a better living situation for everyone. My mother also agreed to stop by once or twice a week to spend time with her father, staying there as long as needed, to allow Anna and Franco to go out for dinner or to the movies. During those times, my father would take care of us and sometimes he would ask his employer if he could leave work earlier. Our home was finally just for us. It did not get bigger; it just seemed bigger and more practical. This was a big accomplishment for my father, all of us, and our extended family that left Tripoli. We were finally living in a better situation than when we arrived. My mother was now alone and more relaxed since Anna was going to take care of their aging father at her house. My mother would sometimes bring me and my sister to visit my grandfather and to offer some support to the aging patriarch. My mother could now fully dedicate herself to raising us and taking care of the family affairs. I was now attending the last year of elementary school, which is the fifth grade.

My father had been working hard for the last four years at the shipyard and he had made quite a name for himself, not only for his expertise but by quickly mastering the production and maintenance aspects of the engines that were powering the state-of-the-art hydrofoils. But with his background of having lived in Tripoli, there was a new trend at work started by his peers to contend with. He was given a nickname by his coworkers; they called him the "Saraceno." In Italian, this term refers to people that belonged to the Arab Middle Eastern region. Even if he was actually not an Arab, but an Italian, they respectfully and in a professional way associate him to the communities where he lived in Libya. It was a fun way for everyone to refer to him by this nickname, which my father did not mind at all. When people wanted to speak with my father at the construction hangers, they would ask, "Have you seen Giorgio Galliani?" They would reply "Who, the Saraceno?" Obviously if any visitors came from the outside, they would be very curious of this nickname. They would be told about my father's time in Libya and that was why he was given that nickname. It was all done in good sportsmanship.

My father had grown quite a reputation of being very analytical and observant, especially when the company conducted live sea trial excursions of all the newly built hydrofoils before being commissioned to the new owners. My father played an active role in making sure that each hydrofoil that was purchased by the clients passed all his mechanical responsibilities. There were very strict tests that were conducted by the company to make sure that each hydrofoil was seaworthy and performed as per the prescribed specifications flawlessly. My father's main responsibility was to make sure that the engines in the newly built hydrofoils achieved all the goals during these sea tests. All the cruising systems and their behavior at sea had to harmoniously interact with all of the other equipment built into this flying ship. I remember my father telling me that some of the sea tests involved the hydrofoil being loaded with mannequins depicting the weight of real passengers. In accomplishing these tests, they would see if the craft behaved correctly even at a full capacity load in any kind of sea conditions. As I said, my father hardly had any engineering education, but he would be very aware and receptive of the way the hydrofoil reacted during these test runs. All of the witnessed mechanical behavior and observations were reported to the engineering staff at the shipyard in charge of the craft design. My father would report his findings mostly in non-engineering terms but also documented by the test instruments that measured the ship dynamics. He would explain to them what he thought needed fine tuning and what was needed because it was not performing as expected. My father's notes and verbal conversations were highly sought, especially if the proposed changes would increase the overall efficiency of the hydrofoil or rectify any experienced vibrations during these tests. What my father reported was not always possible to implement from an engineering perspective since some changes would negatively alter other mechanics or dynamics. But by using some of my father's feedback during the hours spent testing out at sea, the management team became aware of my father's gift that he was able to observe certain behavioral characteristics and report them in laymen's terms. He was not just a highly skilled diesel engine mechanic but also a key component of the building, testing, and maintenance tasks of these hydrofoils. His real-world comments taken into account by the engineers allowed them to fine tune and modify the specifications and also replace some of their materials used.

It was during this time that the Rodriquez Naval Engineering company secured a purchase and delivery contract from the Egyptian government. The Cantieri Navali Rodriquez had to build and deliver several hydrofoils to be used to carry passengers to different cities located along the Nile River. This is the longest river in the world and extends for over 4,000 miles. When these hydrofoils were finally shipped to the Egyptian government, my father together with other key engineers were chosen to fly into Cairo to meet with the government officials and deliver the purchased hydrofoils. My father's role was to teach the local Egyptian naval crews all the mechanical maintenance aspects necessary to correctly run and service their new hydrofoils. He was teamed with a senior captain, part of the Rodriquez family, and his duty was to teach the Egyptian captains how to navigate and maneuver these crafts on the Nile River. The ports on the Nile that needed to be serviced by these hydrofoils were distant from Cairo, the home port. One of these destinations was from Aswan to Abu Simbel, about a 200 Kilometer or 125-mile trip. The hydrofoils with a speed of over forty-five miles per hour would cover the distances in almost one third of the time of the country's traditional ferries.

One of the hydrofoils purchased by the Egyptian government named Nefertiti.

I remember my father explaining to me when I was much older how difficult that work was. He described the brutally hot climate conditions that these hydrofoils were operating under. They required a lot more tender loving care, unlike the ones that were operating in the Italian seas. These hydrofoils were already modified with an expanded cooling system but were still stressed to the max. Due to those African desert temperatures, the engines needed to be cared for with baby gloves. From a mechanical viewpoint, the factory recommended a shortened oil changing cycle due to the hot climate; this put an additional burden on the local maintenance crew. It is important to remember there was no synthetic oil then. My father would also mention the sandstorms that from time to time weathered these parts of the Nile. These sandstorms would partially clog the air filters and other mechanical parts, hindering the operation of some of the hydraulic components of the boat. If these hydrofoils were not properly maintained and inspected frequently in a timely fashion, you could lose an engine, transmission, or the steering capabilities in a heartbeat from the overheating or lack of lubrication.

My father was there for about four months. He went on trips up and down the river on these new hydrofoils with the local mechanics teaching them all these precaution points and procedures. These boats used the best high-powered diesel engines available in those days from Daimler Benz "Germany" and the transmission from ZF, also a German engineering company. For the readers that may own some of the performance cars on the market today such as BMW, Audi, Bentley, and Aston Martin, etc., their performance series also uses some of these components. The engines used in the larger PT50 hydrofoils were twin MB 820 V-12 supercharged diesel engines, while the one in the PT20 was a Daimler-Benz V12 with 1,350 of horsepower. Losing one of these engines would cost an exorbitant amount of money and labor to replace them. They had to follow proper maintenance procedures taught to them by my father or they would fall out of warranty. These stipulations needed to be strictly adhered to, especially in the African heat, or else that probably voided the warranty. Any of these failures would cost hundreds of thousands of dollars. Thus, the manufacturer was really keen on making sure that the end user would follow all the maintenance procedures to the letter. By sending my father with the new hydrofoils, the local mechanical maintenance crew learned how to carry out these maintenance procedures and the timeframes in order to avoid any fatal malfunctions.

Giorgio in Abu Simbel one of the sites serviced by the Hydrofoils about 500 miles south of Cairo on the Nile.

My father was in Egypt in 1963, and very few people in Italy owned or could afford a telephone. We did not have a telephone in our house in Messina. Thus, the only way my father was able to communicate with my mother was via short telegrams. I have seen many of these; they were saved in an old suitcase full of papers and pictures from those times. My father was an avid believer in keeping photographs and old documents as a legacy to his past life in work or pleasure. He probably thought that one day, either his sons or daughter will be able to see and reconnect with him by reviewing those saved documents. That is exactly what I did. His telegrams were very simple, a few words, writing that he was doing okay with his work and hoped that the kids did not miss him too much. The obvious ending words were "Love You, Giorgio." My father sent many of these telegrams to my mother during his stay in Egypt. If I read him correctly, he wanted to make sure that my mother knew that he was always thinking of us and her. Those times must have been hard for my mother with three kids to take care of and no man in the house for months. She found some help from some of our neighbors that knew that my father was working in a faraway country. They would stop by our home on their way out to shop for food, asking her if she needed anything. As you can imagine she could not go anywhere with three kids in the house especially since my younger brother was just one year old. My father's mission came to an end and he was finally back, even if we the kids did not realize he was gone for three or four months. When he returned, I do remember that he took some time off - maybe a couple of weeks. From what I was told, the Rodriquez Company, on top of his regular salary, gave him a bonus for his well accomplished mission in Egypt.

My father decided to put that extra money to good use and bought my mother a washing machine since she was struggling with the laundry. He hired a plumber and electrician to provide the connection in our apartment to hook up the machine. If we revisit a previous portion of this chapter, I mentioned that there was an outside tub located on the veranda to hand wash the family laundry. The problem was that there was no running hot water in those days; this was considered a luxury. The home water heaters were new to the market and very expensive, not to mention the gas expenditure needed to run it. All of the condominiums lacked water heaters. Like everyone else, my mother had to boil water on the stove to use it to take a bath or mix it with the cold water from the faucet to wash ourselves. With the outside tub, my mother washed clothes by hand mostly with cold water. During the winter season, she would use gloves to do the wash, but since the water was much colder in the winter even if her hands were partially protected, she still suffered joint pain by doing the wash in those cold temperature. Obviously with the installation of the washing machine, which also required a hot water hookup from a state-of-the-art hot water heater, the laundry problem was history. This water heater provided hot running water for the bath tub, the outside tub, the kitchen sink, and the newly installed washing machine.

This unit was one of those early gas fired models designed for restricted spaces and efficiency. It would heat up the water as it passed through its twisted tubing surrounded by metal fins directly located over a high natural gas fired flame. We finally had running hot water in our apartment. We could all now enjoy a bath with running hot water on demand. However, I recall that my mother would still enjoy washing the clothing in the outside tub when it was a beautiful and warm day. There was one other catch with this gas fired water heater: it was not automatic. When you needed hot water, you had to turn on the gas pilot unit with a match. This procedure was not for the average homemaker since you had to lift a cover to access the pilot, press, and hold a button while you used a match to light it up. My father mostly attended to that procedure. He would turn the unit on in the morning and my mother would shut it down when the hot water was no longer needed for that day. The two other things that had to be considered was the cost of the gas and the fears to leave the pilot on at all times which could also constitute a fire hazard and a waste of energy. The water heater, once turned on, would deliver hot water just by opening the hot water faucet. The pressure of the water circulating through the fins would fire up the main burner and the water would get hot within a minute.

I know this sounds a little crazy, but we considered ourselves blessed by these opportunities and conveniences that, through my father's hard work, brought these modern-day comforts to our household. These were his gifts to us and he gave us many more throughout his life. Until the time that he died, my father always purchased the latest new appliances, tools, and state of the art electronics as soon as they were available to the general public. Just like the way he was at his job, a kind of a maverick, he would look at any of these new appliances carefully and after careful evaluation and research he would go out and buy them with the extra money that he earned. It may not look like much by today's standards, but life in Italy in the 1960s was not the "Dolce Vita" envisioned in films. Most people lived on a fixed salary and were just getting by every month. You should know that almost everyone received a paycheck once a month, enforcing strict budgeting behavior in order to have the money last until next month's paycheck. I saw my mother micromanage most of the day-to-day monetary needs; my father would only be involved with larger monetary decisions.

Let's get back to my father's work. After he returned from his first Egypt mission, he was even more respected by his co-workers, notwithstanding his blue-collar classification as a diesel mechanic. You may recall that I said earlier that some people thought my father could walk on water; here is one of those examples. The engineering management team was very impressed with my father's growth in knowledge and with his performance. The Cantieri Navali Rodriquez in Messina became kind of a flagship company in Italy for their innovation and state of the art technology in the nation's naval industry. A national syndicated radio program took notice of this and scheduled a live show to be broadcasted directly from inside the shipyard in Messina.

They wanted to do a live interview with key employees and management engineers that made this company a leader in maritime technology in Europe. I believe that due to my father's successful Egyptian missions, with the delivery of the hydrofoils purchased by that government, he was selected by the management to take part in this live radio broadcast. Everyone at the shipyard anticipated this event since it was scheduled weeks in advance. My father asked my mother to record the radio program on his newly purchased German made reel-to-reel voice recorder. This is more proof that my father really liked the new electronic gadgets available during those early technology times. He prepared it for my mother so that all she had to do was to just press the record button. He also instructed us to be quiet during the recording session of the radio show. This particular event exists so freshly in my mind, as if it were yesterday.

It was a big deal to be on the Italian national radio during those years. I remember how my mother and I positioned ourselves around the radio built inside a wooden cabinet along our apartment's short hallway. The recorder was placed next to the radio and the microphone in front of the radio speakers. The atmosphere in my home was electrifying! There was a kind of euphoria all around the apartment. This weekly radio show started at 7:00 PM and lasted one hour. I don't recall if it was a Saturday or Sunday night, but obviously many people that were home during this time would be tuning in from all around the country. I recall that once we heard the initial soundtrack from the program, my mother pushed the button so that the whole broadcast could be fully recorded. We had this tape for many decades but, unfortunately, it was probably lost in one of our relocations. I wish I could still hear it today.

I recall seeing the red recording light come on and then everyone was quiet. The host introduced the location of his live broadcast to the Italian radio audience. The announcer did his initial introduction saying that "We are broadcasting live from the Rodriquez shipyard in Messina." He explained what the company did and that the hydrofoils were manufactured right inside the hangers from where they were located during this live broadcast.

He narrated a brief history of the company from its very beginnings and that of the owners. He also expanded on the number of employees currently working there and that everyone was a highly skilled engineer, technician or mechanic: "Everyone here works as a team to build these fantastic ships called the hydrofoils." He followed his presentation by detailing that he would be speaking directly with some key employees that were part of the company's success story. "These technicians and engineers," he explained, "that work here will tell us about their skills and responsibilities. This will help us understand some very interesting facts about these hydrofoils and why this company is such a pacesetter in our country." He also forewarned that he would interview some fascinating individuals that are the heart of this company: "These professionals will also tell us a little bit about themselves and their background and some of them have a really interesting personal history." As soon as I heard that, I instantly thought that he was probably referring to my father since he was the one that came from another country, and given a funny nickname. The program started by first interviewing the management team, which included the owners and the designing team of engineers. As time passed, I was anxiously waiting to hear my father's voice. The show had gone for forty-five minutes so far, and my father had not been on the radio yet. "Would there be time left for him," I wondered.

After the last commercial, the host finally introduced my father. The host introduced him as a special personage, noting that "not only he is one of the key engine mechanics that works here, but he also brings with him something very unusual in his background. I would like our radio audience to know that he is known by his colleagues with a nickname in the Cantieri Rodriquez. They sometimes call him 'the Saraceno.' I want to introduce to you 'Il signor Giorgio Galliani.'" I could hear all the other workers congregating around him, whistling and cheering with exultation when his name was announced. It felt to me that the host had just introduced some kind of movie star. However, in reality, it was just my father: the hard-working mechanic for the Cantieri Rodriquez. But for that moment, my father became my "John Wayne" or "Frank Sinatra." The first thing, obviously, that the host asked him was, "Tell us why they call you the 'Saraceno.' When he started talking, I did not recognize his voice. It sounded very young and a little metallic, probably due to the radio broadcasting equipment used in those days. It also appeared that he had a slight foreign accent compared to the people previously interviewed. Those people enunciated the words and verbs very well. I could tell that my father was your average 'Giorgio' in that group, but he was not afraid or ashamed to show it.

My father's first response was to explain his nickname. He told the audience that his family came from Tripoli, Libya, the Italian colony where he grew up. He explained that due to that city's location in the northern part of Africa, "They playfully assume that I belonged to some Arab tribe, so my coworkers gave me that nickname." I distinctly recall hearing the background on the radio, again the cheers and whistles from his co-workers when my father said that. I thought to myself, "Wow! My father must be really liked and respected by them to cheer him on so much, and definitely more than the others that were previously interviewed." The rest of the discussion was about his job and what his responsibilities as part of the engine mechanical team in the shipyard looked like. He spoke for about five minutes and did not miss a beat or make any mistakes. It reminded me of my Christmas performance in church a year or so back, in front of all those people. But my father was heard by many thousands if not a million people throughout Italy.

I was glad that he had the opportunity to be on that show. I was so very proud of him and from that time on, he would always be my superstar. Maybe he could actually walk on water. I wish today that I could have told him that many times, but unfortunately, I did not do it enough. Why do we regret these things? Like not saying "I love you" until after people die. I will never understand that, but it happens to so many of us.

When I was in my 30s, I asked my father what he felt when he was interviewed on that radio program. "Did you feel overwhelmed with emotions and fearful when the moment came for your interview?" I asked. He told me that "When you believe in yourself and know your job well, the words come out freely, easily, and correctly." I also asked: "Did you feel intimidated being interviewed on a national radio show? Did you feel like you were not very important, since all the others that were interviewed were engineers or architects with a college education or degree?" He said "Son" translated from Italian. He would always start with this Italian word many times when he wanted to make a real point with me: "Figlio." "When you know that you are standing on solid ground with both of your two feet well planted and you also know that you have done your job to the best of your abilities you will have no reservations. Remember the time when you were very young and the nun put you in front of all those people in church? Well, how did you feel? You executed your mission without missing a beat. I was there in the back of the church and I was real proud of your performance. Always take the bull by the horn and do not let it go until you conquer him. You will feel in power and you will be the winner. Always make sure that you execute well to the best of your abilities with no excuses and with all the tools that have been given to you. Then, you will experience no fear."

There is an important person whom I must acknowledge at this point. His name was Pippo and he was also employed by the Rodriquez Company as a mechanic's apprentice. He was ten years younger than my father and he eventually became one of my father's best friends. The last time I spoke to him he was still living in the city of Messina. I was able to trace him down by using the internet and searching the phone directories in Messina since I also knew his last name. He quickly recognized me on the very first phone call. During this initial conversation, he became very emotional, especially after we started to talk about my father after so many decades. He said that he needed to get a glass of water to calm him down and that he was also taking blood pressure medication and did not want to get too excited. Our exchanges and his recollections from my questions became a little overwhelming for him at times; he was now in his eighties. I could tell from his responses that he really respected my father. He eventually calmed down and began to enjoy our conversation. We talked a few other times in the following weeks. My main goal was to get an inside view of my father at his job and what was it like to work with him for so many years. We talked about his day-to-day interactions with my father during the work day. Pippo explained to me that during the course of all those years, he was blessed to have worked under my father's wings. He also recounted that both of them, together, became a great mechanical team at the shipyard. He told me that when he first met my father he was a young, inexperienced, and unschooled person needing a mentor. Like my father, he also loved to work on engines and other mechanical gears. He was willing just to hand him the tools that my father needed, observe his work, and learn as much as he could initially. "Your father," he said, "was very organized. He wanted his work area nice and clean all the time. That for me was an experience in itself. I was hired as a mechanical apprentice at the shipyard; when your father started working there, the company assigned me to be mostly his mechanical assistant." Pippo said that he started working at Rodriquez in 1956 when he was only sixteen years old, which was a few years before my father arrived. "I wanted to learn the trade and, frankly speaking," he said to me, "I could not have found a better teacher than your father." I asked Pippo many times to describe what it was like to work with my father, and he was in ecstasy recalling those moments and days.

> *"Most of the days," he said, "we just repaired broken engines with minor issues, but sometimes we had to rebuild the whole engine. We had to take apart every piece of that powerful engine and rebuild it with new parts from the ground up. This job would take a month or more depending on the availability of the parts that needed to be replaced. I can only swear to you that when I and your father were finished rebuilding that engine, it would run like it was brand new from the factory. Your father had a special gift when it came to rehabilitating a broken engine and all the other associated parts that propelled those hydrofoils. You know, these boats raced above the sea level at speeds of more than forty knots. Sometimes he wanted to double check his work and would make me take apart some of the already assembled portions, because he personally wanted to double verify that they met the manufacturer's specifications. He would re-measure those new parts installed and only once he validated the measurements, I would be able to put it back together."*

I am sure that my readers are familiar with the old carpenter's rule "Measure twice and cut only once." I guess my father followed this rule even with his trade. Pippo continued on:

> *"He would explain to me why he was so detailed and careful in his work. 'I want you, Pippo, to know that this engine is worth a lot of money and the company*

> *pays us to make sure it will be as good as new once it is rebuilt. These engines are made to last thousands of hours of normal operation when they came to us new from the factory. When we rebuild them, this shipyard trusts us to deliver them as good as they were when they were new. The sea does not forgive and if any of our engines fails during a trip, it could spell disaster. People's lives are at stake even on a short thirty minute trip; there is always the chance that something will go wrong. My responsibility is to make sure that my engines, once re-installed on the boat, will perform and last as prescribed. This is why I want to check everything twice to make sure that I have done my best on this job."*

Pippo went on to tell me of many events during my father's work, such as how he would engage with the mechanical engineers that were designing the hydrofoils' mechanical layout. "One time," he said, "some engineers questioned your father's observations taken during the test runs that would certify the hydrofoil for final delivery and to be put in commercial use." One of his recollections was an episode that took place during one of these many test runs being carried out on the Strait of Messina. The hydrofoil showed some unexpected vibrations when it reached a certain speed, but it then faded and went away as the boat accelerated. He told to me that "Your father would explain to the Engineers, that there was something missing or not properly accounted for in their calculations with the design mechanism of the propulsion engines." My father's comments were very upsetting to the engineering staff, especially since it was brought up by a technician or, in their minds, just by an engine mechanic. My father would explain to them that his observations were based on all of his years of experience and from his own point of view. He would tell them that it is up to them to make the modification needed to resolve the issue that he was describing. He would say to them:

> *"I am sure that the problem is not with my engines or the transmission for which I am responsible, they are all performing as expected. I believe it is something in the way we transmit the power to the propellers, something needs to be modified somewhere between the engine, the transmission, or the propellers. These vibrations are only noticeable at a particular power band range of the engines and at a particular torque transmission point."* Pippo said that *"I would just listen quietly during these discussions between him and the engineers. I could not believe that your father was so sure of his findings. He also was very receptive of the engineers' reactions and attitude, they acted like master designers with their big piece of degree in advanced mechanical engineering and mathematical computation skills. To this day, I can only tell you that your father would substantiate his argument from his notes that he took during these test runs. Your father knew what he was talking about and he was sure he had taken the correct annotations. When we finally left that meeting, I observed a couple of design engineers just shaking their heads. They were confident from their point of view since it was verified by the engineering tests and data design that did not support any fault in their construction.*

One week after the event above, your father learned from the other group of mechanics that were taking care of the propeller system that they were told to replace some of the bushing bearings. These bearings guided the power from the engine transmission driveshaft to the propellers. They were replaced with stronger and larger capacity bushing units. Low and behold, on our next sea test run, all the previous vibrations disappeared. Your father was right, it had nothing to do with the engine. He said that the news spread quickly but quietly around the shipyard. Your father became their engineer without a degree, not just a diesel mechanic." Pippo said *"I was so proud to be working with him. Your father was a true thinker and solved many other problems by applying his acquired knowledge and experience to real life difficulties. The only things that your father lacked was that college degree. However, if you really want to know it did not mean much to me. I always looked up to him as my mentor. Your father was prepared with real world experience and his logical mind allowed him to solve complex mechanical engineering issues. When your family left to go to America, I lost not only my best teacher but also my great friend. After he left, I was able to proceed and exceed in my work because I learned so much from him, by paying real attention every single day I worked with him. But I had to fill very big shoes and sometimes I wished that he was still with me at the shipyard. I survived and actually exceeded my responsibilities, thanks to your father, until the shipyard silently moved on to other ventures. I want to let you know, that after almost forty years working there, those years with your father were the best years and times of my life. I was blessed to have known your father, Giorgio."*

The new generation of hydrofoils built after my father left Messina.

This is where I want to bring to light my own and best treasured day spent with my father during my childhood. The reason why it is lengthy and so detailed is because this event is still so fresh in my heart and my mind, as if it happened yesterday. It also brings nostalgic memories of my father during that period where he exposed his true spirit and his caring ways to show me what he really was made of. An analogous event like this one will never happen again between us.

I was probably eleven years old at that time. It was a beautiful late spring or early summer day in the city of Messina, likely a Saturday afternoon.

My father was not wearing his usual work outfit: just regular pants, a shirt and a heavy sport jacket. I am sure that there must have been some kind of interesting dialogue with my mother where he must have said to her that he wanted to bring me out with him on one of the hydrofoils. She came to my room and told me to put a pullover over my shirt because I was going with my father on a little trip and it might be a little chilly where he was taking me. As you know by now, my father liked to go out on trips with all of us as a family unit. I was a little surprised that he just wanted me to be with him this time. I had never been alone on an outing just with him. I was so excited that I speedily put the extra clothing on so that I could be quickly on my way.

I followed him to the front door while my mother held my hand and said to me "You make sure that you stay next to your father and follow to the word anything that he says." This was very unusual that she would remind me of that, because I always did just that. As we got into the car, he said that we were going to the Port of Messina, where we were going to go out on one of the company hydrofoils for a short trip at sea. I could not hold my excitement when I heard that! My father was going to take me on one of the ships that he works on! I felt like I just became a man in that instant.

The short drive to the city harbor only took about ten minutes and we parked the car in a private spot marked for his company's use. There were several huge commercial ships anchored all along the pier followed by a couple of smaller government "Vedettes" or what we know in America as the Coast Guard boats. Very close to where we parked, a couple of hydrofoils were also floating next to the pier wall. A chill went up and down my spine. I had never been onboard any of my father's ships but today was going to be that day.

As we approached the two ships, one of them looked like nobody was onboard, but on the other, I could see three people moving around on the top. My father was holding my hand as we walked over to that one and said to me, "You need to be near or next to me at all times unless I tell you otherwise and do exactly what I tell you to do." I told him "Si Papa." As we walked toward that particular hydrofoil with the people onboard, I noticed that he was wearing his work shoes not his dress shoes. I thought instantly, "Is he taking me to work with him?" But this was not the shipyard where they built them, we were at the harbor. As we arrived next to that boat, a steel bridge was in place across the edge of the water wall and the boat. Two sailors, that is what I called them, were waiting at the end of that bridge platform on the boat and waived us through.

As we stepped foot on that ship, I felt like a really important person. I felt like I was in heaven. At the same time, my throat clamped down, and I could hardly swallow. The sailors saluted my father by saying "Good day, Signor Galliani. Welcome onboard." One of them said to him, "Well, it is about time that you bring your son to see what you do for work." I was flabbergasted and feeling like I was the son of one of the greatest naval Admirals in the world stepping on his flag ship. But, on the other hand, I was just with my father. From the control room located just two steps up to the left of a steel platform, a man in full naval officer uniform came to greet us. I could not take much more of this excitement. It was an overwhelming experience and I was not ready to experience all of this at once.

This individual was addressed by my father as "Captain" with a name that I do not recall. It was noticeable that this man was already a longtime friend of my father. They must have known each other for years, and no formalities were needed here. "Wow," I said to myself, "My father really walks the high ground and now also the high seas for sure." The Captain said to my father "Signor Galliani! Nice to see you again! Is this your young son?" My father said, "Yes, this is Giuseppe, my eldest one. As you know, I also have a younger daughter and another baby boy." "Congratulations to you," the Captain said. "Your son looks like he is going to follow in his father's footsteps." My father replied, "Well, he needs to study hard first, find out what it is in his heart and follow his own path. If this what he likes to do, I think this work would suit him quite nicely." He also said to him, "Please call me 'Giorgio.' We are here to do a little bit of observation and maybe some work next week." The Captain replied "Si, Signor Giorgio, let's go and see how good this hydrofoil handles himself where it counts." Again, I said to myself, "He didn't understand my father! He still addressed him as 'Signor.' He must have really had a high level of respect for my dad!

As the captain turned on the ship engines, the smell of diesel fuel filled the air. The engines below began to softly roar and the ship pushed off the port wall with the help of the other two sailors. I could feel a small vibration below my feet. My father asked me to sit on a small leather covered foldable chair that he pulled up right outside the entrance of the Captain's Navigation Bridge. He secured a belt around my waist and asked me to stay there and enjoy the ride. I was facing the rear of the open ship, which is called the starboard side, and I had an incredible view of the Port of Messina as we were pulling away from it. I could see brown smoke on the back of the hydrofoil from the exhaust pipe somewhere below starboard. This was a typical hydrofoil with a front cabin below and a smaller cabin in the back. The two cabins could carry many passengers, which made you feel like you were sitting in a jet airplane. My father went inside the control cabin with the Captain and was talking to him. The sound of the engine was overtaking their conversation since I was sitting outside. The other two people were doing things around the boat. They were moving as if the boat was docked. Obviously, they were experienced sailors and knew the ship inside out; nothing bothered them. From my viewpoint, I could see us slowly leaving the port as the homes and buildings on the mainland were getting smaller and farther away.

My mother was right: I did need an extra layer. It feels a lot colder out to sea than when you are on land, even in the early summer. My father checked on me to make sure all was fine. I was so overwhelmed by the experience that I could hardly talk, but I nodded my head. One of the two sailors came on the platform where I was sitting and a few feet away toward the back portion, he unlocked a large floor panel or bulkhead, then pulled it open. As soon as that happened, the sound of the engines became much louder. "That must be the engine's access door," I thought to myself. This opening was big enough for an adult to fit nicely through. As the boat was cutting through the water at low speed with its wings still under the sea, the waves produced by the sheer size of the floating body were splashing softly against the steel hull. The squishing sound of the water as it moved around the outside body of the ship was a reminder that we were going into deeper water. The sea was pretty calm and we were almost a couple hundred yards going outside the harbor heading to the open sea. My father walked over to the bulkhead opening, turned himself around facing me while holding onto a floor support and he started going down inside that hole. "There must be stairs," I said to myself which carried him below and he quickly disappeared inside the boat's bowels. I don't know what he was doing in there, but I figured he was checking the engines to make sure everything looked normal in there. As the hydrofoil heads to open waters, the engines are usually pushed to their full power. This creates the lift necessary by its wings to bring the hull above the water as it rides on these special wings attached underneath. This allows the craft to achieve its cruising speed of around 45 knots or about 50 miles per hour.

While I was sitting several feet from that opening, I heard my father call one of the sailors attending the boat from below. As this person came to my father, they spoke and then he turned around, walked toward me and said, "Your father asked me to help you to go below; he wants to show you the engines." When he told me that, I was stunned and very much afraid of what was going to occur. I could not believe what was happening to me. As I left the safety of the chair and walked a couple of steps with this gentleman's help to that opening, I saw my father below in a large opening standing up below on that floor. It was not that deep, maybe a little more than eight or nine feet, but to me it was menacing. My father asked me to come down the steps attached to the wall and he guided my feet until I also reached the bottom. He gave me some earmuffs to blunt some of the engine noises, which made a noticeable difference to me. There were large, covered exhaust pipes that ran outside the hydrofoil, which added to the engines sound. I had no fear once I was next to my father. I was sure that he had been there hundreds of times before. I was standing on that floor that vibrated from the engines running a couple of feet to my right and to my left. We were both in an empty working space between these two beautiful V12 Mercedes Diesel engines. They were purring just like big cats do, but I could feel their awesome presence of power if unleashed, a really toxic experience. I asked my father about two large snail like structures on the top side of each engine and wanted to know what they were. He told me that those units are what gives the engine the extra power that is needed to lift the craft out of the water. They are called turbochargers and they compress additional air inside the engine combustion to increase the horsepower output of each engine. While I was admiring all the mechanical technology of that era present inside the body of that beautiful ship, the Captain came over the top to talk to my father. He said to him "Signor Giorgio, are we ready to lift this boat out of the water?" My father replied, "Everything looks good here. Please help my son back above and place him on the chair that he was on." The Captain helped me back up and put me back on my seat. He went back to my father and said, "Signor Giorgio, would you like to come up here and drive her? So, you can evaluate her in how she lifts out of the water?"

I could not believe my ears; the Captain wanted my father to drive the hydrofoil so he could feel and see for himself that all the systems functioned as expected! "Wow!" I said to myself, "The Captain really respected my father's experience and mechanical knowledge." "You know" he said to my father, "I am the Captain but you are the master of these engines; if they don't work as expected I don't know what to do, that is where you come in." My father replied to him, "Captain, you just let me know the engine readings from your gauges in real time. I think I can best evaluate the mechanics from here below. If I see or hear anything out of the normal, I can best evaluate it by being right next to the engine." They agreed and now all was in place for this ship to take off, much like a plane does as it builds speed on the asphalt runway.

My sensations were now culminating in a ball of emotional fire. I felt very afraid of this event that was going to take place because I never experienced it before. I said to myself, "Nothing bad is going to happen here, I am around the most professional people that you can have, and one of them is my father. Sit back, hold tight, and enjoy the ride of your life." As the Captain accelerated, the purring engines' sound became more like wild cats increasing their roar as they were chasing their prey. The hydrofoil's speed increased as the sea water splashed on its hull. I could see a white foam trail being generated behind the boat as the sea's water was displaced. I was pushed back into my chair and glad that I had my security belt firmly on. I was very impressed that the other two sailors were just standing and holding on to the outside rails of the boat. It looked like they were enjoying the ride and were quite comfortable with their feet solidly planted on the hull floor. The captain was announcing the engine's Revolutions Per Minute (RPMs) to my father below as they appeared on his gauge. I am sure that he must have taken his ear muffs off in order to hear the Captain's numbers. My father answered him loudly by saying to him, "Let me know when we are approaching two thousand RPMs; the boat should lift out of the water." The captain yelled, "Yes, Signor Galliani, we are at one thousand-five hundred now, and I am accelerating." The captain started to loudly say "1600, 1700, 1800. I see the boat lifting. 1900, 2000. We are now out of the water, Giorgio." "Wow," I said to myself in the excitement, "He forgot the 'Signor.'"

From my take, I could not believe how this mighty ship was now flying above the waves so smoothly and so fast. Both the front and rear wings were above the water holding this craft well above the surface and cruising at an incredible speed that I never imagined. My father came out of that space now and stepped into the control room with the Captain. He must be checking all the gauges that relayed all the statistics about the hydrofoils and, most important, that of the engines. The Captain was driving this boat just like he was an airplane pilot and, at that speed, the reaction times are very much compacted. I am sure his eyes were very focused on the sea in front and to the sides of him in order to react promptly to any issues. Almost five minutes had gone by and the wind generated by the speed on the outside of this craft was such a new experience for me, as hats would be flying out to sea if you had one. What a sobering experience I was having, but everyone else seemed very much accustomed to it, just like another day at the park.

After traveling about ten minutes in a straight forward direction the Captain said "Okay, let's turn her around and head her back to the port." You are probably thinking at that speed this hydrofoil covers a lot of distance in that timeframe. The port could be seen very slightly in the distance; we did cover a lot of sea since our departure. The return for me was the enjoyable part since I was now more relaxed because my father stepped out of the control room and was now next to me. As we turned around he pointed out some of the landmarks onshore that I was familiar with when we travelled in our car. The perception of those places from the sea was quite amazingly different from the overall notion of driving on land. We were about a mile from land and running parallel to the city beaches. We went by some fishing boats in the distance and there was also a large commercial ship about a mile away. It is very hard to judge distance when you are out to sea. The speed of the hydrofoil also makes it even harder as the sea water flows by so fast. I was glad that my father took the time during the trip back to be near me and to point out things that will be ever present in my life. The sailor closed the bulk head door to the engine room as we were heading back home.

The mission was a great success and everything performed as expected. Even the Captain, whom I could see through the glass windows of his console, was having a well-deserved cigarette which he also offered to my father as he stepped out. Yes, my father smoked in those days and many years after that, not a chain smoker, maybe two packs a week. This was not a great habit since today we all know the consequences. Myself, I smoked a little bit when I attended college but maybe one or two cigarettes a day; not really a habit, but still a smoking dilemma.

As we approached the harbor, the engines' speed was reduced and the speed decelerated. As the speed and power dropped, the lift was reduced and the hull of the hydrofoil sunk back into the water. The vessel now looked and moved just like any other small ship in the water. The water channel entrance to the Port of Messina is slightly narrow and speeds need to be obeyed so that no accident occurs with any of the other boats navigating the strait. The approach to the dock is where the Captain's skills really stand out; he has to use both engines in a non-mirrored fashion to slowly coast next to the wall. As it was expected, this Captain was a real pro. I am sure he had already done this hundreds of times. As the hydrofoil came to almost a stop, a rope was thrown to an additional person on the dock. Once the boat was secured, we were fully parked. As the sailor prepared the bridge to get off the boat, my father exchanged greetings with the Captain and said that he would see him during the week at the shipyard. The Captain also approached me and said, "I hope that you enjoyed the trip and that you will come again with your father." I was going to shake his hand, but the Captain saluted me by bringing his right hand and upper arm horizontal to his forehead, as is customary by a ship official. I replied with the same salute to him. I guess I am now an indoctrinated and sanctioned child that has survived the most incredible lifetime experience of his youth. As we drove back home, my father asked me if I liked being on the boat and at sea. I told him that I will never forget it for the rest of my life. I had just witnessed how my father really earned his money and it wasn't for the fainthearted.

It was now 1965 and I finally graduated from the Catholic elementary school. My parents opted to enroll me in one of the public schools about a mile walk from our home. This school offered the 6th to 8th grade classes, which is Italy's secondary school grades. These three years of school would prepare you for either the pre-college school, better known here as the "High School" or a trade school. Boy, what a rude awakening that was. I was almost ten years old, one year younger than most of my schoolmates, and I suddenly realized that I became in charge of my own learning destiny. These grades demanded a lot more responsibilities than one could have imagined, especially since I was coming from a Catholic elementary school. The first thing that struck me was the lack of supervision for your attendance to the courses. It was pretty much your choice whether to show up for the classes or not. In the 1960s, the curriculum for the 6th grade was preselected and included the dreaded Latin language. The core subjects were Italian, Algebra, a foreign language ("English" in my case), Science, History, and Physical Education. The best thing about this curriculum was that you would go to school on the days and times when your courses were offered. The main reason why I attended a public school, I can speculate, could have been related to some family financial difficulties prioritizing where the fixed income should be spent. The school, unfortunately, did not provide any textbooks. Before the school year started, a list of books for each class was posted at the main entrance, along with the bookstores carrying them in the city. These books were somewhat expensive if new, but if you were lucky and quick to act, a previous year student would sell them to you used at a substantial discount. Our household now had two other young children and we had many more expenses to be accounted for, so if you could secure them used, this was the way to go.

The Italian curricula of the median grade schools may look more similar to our High School courses in the United States, but remember I was only in the 6th grade. The Italian national school system of those days was setup so that each student had to attend a total of twenty-five hours per week of classes. The national counsel expected each student to attend weekly: six hours for Italian, three hours for mathematics, four hours for History/ Geography, two hours of foreign language, etc. Like I said, your attendance was not so obligatory, but if you missed any of these classes you were looking at a rather long catch up time. The professor would explain some of the key topics in the class environment with examples and discussions. If you had to tackle the book on your own, it was an uphill battle unless you were very bright or had someone at home to help you.

I remember the feeling on that first day at my new school. For the first time in my life, I felt afraid of going to this school. The building was three times bigger than my old elementary school and the teachers were now professors, not nuns. I walked to school on that first day on my own from our condominium. That feeling in me must be analogous of a bird when it flies out from his nest for the very first time. The stress and expectations placed upon me in this new school setting provided me with my first realization, which was that from now on I would be in charge of my responsibilities from a schooling perspective.

When I made it to the school, we waited outside until the morning class was called in session. I saw the older boys and girls that were starting their last year at this school, the 8th graders, as strong examples of what was to come. They looked confident, affluent, and depicted a sense of being very independent. This exposure gave me a sense of self accomplishment. I was on my way now to make a real difference in the world. To be honest, I never experienced that feeling again until I enrolled in my first year of college in the United States.

Somehow, the Italian educational system was designed to bestow much responsibility to students at a much younger age than the American pre-college school system. It is no coincidence that with this kind of educational system, you mature much faster than you probably should. What I also realized was that my parents became more hands off from their previous role of just one year earlier. But this feeling was also short lived and bittersweet, due to the fact that the new school academic agenda was very demanding. I understood soon enough that even by attending all the classes that there was much more homework and reading to do after school. I was given some heads up by reading the school newspapers and I also recalled my fifth-grade teacher describing how things would be much more demanding next year. She used to say to us, "If you think that I am giving you a lot of homework, wait until you see what is waiting for you next year." She was completely correct and so were the articles that I read in the newspaper. I became friendly with other boys that attended this school and discovered that they also lived in my same condominium complex but they were assigned to a different study section.

After the first week of classes, I realized that studying together with those other students on some subjects could be beneficial to learning and to executing the homework much more efficiently. I asked my mother if I could go over to their home to study together in the afternoon, so that we could help each other. The real reason, actually, was that my home was not a good learning space and it was very hard to concentrate on my new school work. There was too much noise made by my younger brother and sister, as they liked to play in the afternoons while my studies required silence. My mother gave me the okay only after she made sure that my new friends' parents did not mind me being there. Their home was in the same building but had a different entrance about 100 feet away from ours. What I really liked about their home was that their parents had separated their living room with a small, closed study space. One of these friends was named Rosario. He was actually the youngest in the house; his sister was much older and there was absolute peace and quiet during the afternoons. I went over to Rosario's house probably twice a week. We studied together and helped each other to solve mathematical problems and to write essays for English literature. Our homework time was in the afternoon for about two or three hours. Rosario's mother was very nice and made me feel comfortable and welcomed. After we finished, and if the weather permitted, we would go and play some soccer in the enclosed playground behind the building. We called this outdoor space in Italian "Il cortile."

Dinnertime was around 7:30 PM or 8:00 PM at my home. My father would come back from work around 6:30 PM or 7:00 PM, but I made sure that I would be back home before him. You see, my father was old fashioned; hard to explain it nowadays, but he wanted to see everyone home when he came back from work. I guess he also wanted me to be with the right people and always thought that in every crowd there was a bad apple. I think that he hardly knew that I would go over to my friend's house to study and my mother kept that between us.

I have no proof of this, but when he was very young during the war he may have had some negative encounters with strangers. Unfortunately, I was never able to discuss his tenure of those days since the subject never came out. To this day, I am sorry and feel guilty that I never reflected more on this or asked him why he was so protective of me during those early years in Italy. We all have regrets after dear people like our parents die. We must be more inquisitive because time waits for no one. We only recognize our lost opportunities when it is too late and those opportunities already passed you by. I feel that in writing this book my soul is somewhat nurtured with a conciliatory feeling that flushes out some of my repentances. My true recollections of him and other members of my family act like a vaccine for my past self-inflicted wounds.

In those early years, my father was also commissioned by his company to travel and work in other cities within Italy where some of the hydrofoils operated. These trips, unlike the Egyptian trips, were relatively short - no more than a few days - just enough time to make repairs needed or to conduct key maintenance routines if no qualified staff was available. I retained some black and white photos of him during a special trip outside Italy to enhance his knowledge, sponsored by the Rodriquez shipyard. This trip together with other engineers was to the city of Stuttgart, Germany. The objective of these trips was to get the latest mechanical training for the engines and transmissions manufactured in the plant of Benz and ZF. As I wrote earlier, the hydrofoils' propulsion system was powered either by a single or dual Mercedes diesel engine. The horsepower from the engines was conveyed via a ZF manufactured transmission to the hydrofoil's propellers. These trips were crucial in order to stay on top of the latest improvements by these two German manufacturers.

I was amazed later in my life when I was able to see some pictures from those trips, in one of his photo albums. What I noticed in these photos, and it was very striking to me, was that my father was actually wearing a suit and a black thin tie notorious of the 1960s. As I have mentioned through the book, my father would be seen wearing a mechanic's one-piece jumpsuit most of the time and I always imagined him that way. If you looked at those photos and didn't know anything about my father, you would assume from those photographs that he was an executive or an engineer for the company.

The engineering team from the shipyard that went on these trips was made up of seasoned middle-aged men. In the photos, my father was definitely the youngest person there. I guess he must have been thirty-five years old by then, and he was quite handsome by today's standards. This event further reinforced the important position that my father was seen playing in the success during those early years of the Rodriquez Company. Unfortunately, my father wasn't wearing a suit in the pictures of the other trips, especially when he travelled to the northern part of Italy. This was because he was there to make repairs to the hydrofoils. But looking at some postcard from that part of Italy, one of these places was on the Lake of Garda, the largest lake in Italy located just east of Milan. It measures thirty-two miles long and ten miles wide and it spans across two of the Italian northern regions. On this lake, two important tourist cities, Limone and Garda, are located along the lakeshore lines and the hydrofoil serviced them daily. I am not sure whom he traveled with in those days, but I am sure that his assistant helped in getting those hydrofoils back in operation in a very short time. He managed to always find the time to enjoy these excursions as much as possible, documented by pictures at tourist attractions and restaurants within that region of Italy, or outside the country far away from home. "You see," my father always said to me, "that if you love your work you do not consider it as work." I guess it is true from the well-known statement that, if you "choose a job you love, you will never have to work a day in your life." I can be a testimony to that. I have witnessed my father hundreds of times with his hands dirty and greasy. He never once complained because his work gave him a feeling of satisfaction and accomplishment. However, he also said many times to me, that it would be better for me to learn a job where you do not get your hands and clothing so dirty. With that said, he would follow it by saying to me, "I did not have the opportunity to attend college, but my hands took me far more than I would have imagined." He also went many days on several occasions to Naples, for minor repairs or to provide local training to the support staff there. The company sold several hydrofoils to the Italian government in order to provide fast water transportation between key tourist spots. These well-known islands were Capri and Ischia, and service was provided from the mainland in Naples. These islands were, and they still are, a touristic high spot due to their beauty and location in the middle of the Tyrrhenian Sea. This fast connectivity by sea provided by the hydrofoil allows tourists to spend more time on the islands instead of traveling there via a slow ferry boat. The company would dispatch what I call the "Dynamic Mechanic Duo:" Giorgio and his assistant, Pippo, from their Messina shipyard to service these spots.

Unfortunately, some of these trips were overshadowed by the local work done in Messina at the shipyard. This usually would happen when a large commercial ship experienced a mechanical failure within the Strait of Messina and was towed to the Port of Messina. The Rodriquez Company was the only qualified contractor for these marine jobs that employed the best and experienced marine engine mechanics in the city. Very often, my father was called with his crew to make these repairs on these large commercial ships towed and then anchored in the Port of Messina. Many of these ships were from foreign nations and carried goods to be delivered to their final destination. When the Rodriquez Company was contracted to make these repairs, they would send their available mechanics on board these vessels. This took them away from their day-to-day work at home in the shipyard. They would work around the clock day and night to complete these repairs in order to get the ship back to sea so that it could continue on to its final destination.

Many times, my father was put in charge of this repair crew and he would spend much time on the large ships to make sure that the work was completed correctly, swiftly, and on-time. I remember him on many of those occasions coming home late at night maybe 11:00 PM or midnight and saying that he had to be back on the job by 7:00 AM the next morning. My mother always had dinner set aside and ready for him. I tried to stay up as much as possible and if I was still awake in my bedroom, I would go to the kitchen and hug him and just watch. He would say to me "Go back to bed. It is late for you. You have to be in school tomorrow morning." I can still remember today, more than fifty years later, that unique odor of his mechanic work outfit. It was a mix of diesel fumes and motor oil. Even if my father washed his hands and changed his clothes at work before coming home, he would still bring that particular scent that he absorbed just by working around the engines all day. That scent even today reminds me of him, especially if I am at an auto repair shop or other places where vehicles are being serviced. The same odor brings back those times when my father would come home, most unmistakably, from those late nights at work.

This brings me to an interesting story about my father. He was a very finicky eater, probably due to my mother's excellent cooking. She spoiled him, so obviously he did not like to buy prepared food. He would come home starving at times since he had not eaten all day. The last time he probably ate was that morning and that was what I call his daily peasant breakfast, consumed before he went to work, usually around 7:00 AM. What was that breakfast for my father? Italian hard-crusted bread leftover from a couple of days. This bread would be slightly dry but not too hard; he would break it up with his fingers in small bite size pieces and place it all in a large bowl. My mother would prepare an espresso coffee pot, mix it with hot milk and pour it on top of these pieces of bread. Sprinkle a little bit of sugar on top, mix it, let it stand for a minute and that was his breakfast early in the morning. This was almost a daily ritual. If bread was unavailable, my mother would have some hard homemade cookies which replaced the bread. However, he liked the bread the most and would actually find it most of the time due to my mother's diligence. Sometimes there would be some pasta left over from the night before and that would be his lunch that he would take with him. Unfortunately, when he was working under those very demanding situations he sometimes forgot to eat and that was why he would come home starving. If you walked into our home and looked on top of our kitchen stove or inside the refrigerator, fresh daily cooked food was always readily available. If my father missed dinner with us, it would be waiting for him on his arrival.

I fondly remember about thirty-five years ago when I first started working on my own in the computer consulting business, one of my first clients was a machine shop that needed my early computer software expertise. When I entered that shop for the first time to meet with the owner at his office, I clearly recalled the same odor and scents of motor oil coming from his shop machinery just a few feet away behind a door. The machine shop was right next to his office partition. I found myself in heaven being able to work in that environment; the odors always reminded of those days with my father. I never told him of that experience, even if he was much older and we were living in the United States when he was working for a large trucking company. I loved to work at this client's shop and be able to walk in his machine shop. I was helping him to design the early database programs of the 1980s to keep track of his jobs on his newly purchased IBM personal computer. The real difference was that I used my brain to program the software and my hands to come in contact with the computer keyboard. Unlike my father, I never came in contact with any mechanical gears or motors but enjoyed the feeling that this machine shop environment gave me during my work there.

In 1966, our family had to endure the passing of both of my grandfathers: Vincenzo and Giuseppe. It was a bad year for everyone. I call them the patriarchs of our family. The roots that they planted were very crucial in shaping my life and generations to come. They were part of what the United States calls the Greatest Generation. I belong to the Baby Boomer generation. Even if I lived my younger days in a foreign country, I identify myself with the Baby Boomer generation's ideals, principles, and achievements. My grandparents had done all they could after the second world war for their son and daughters in order to have the opportunity to form their own family in that new era of peace and financial stability. With their passing, our family experienced a closure of their contributions and of that generation.

During that year while in 6th grade, it became very hard for me to concentrate on my schoolwork. It was not only due to losing my grandparents but also that I became more mature and that I was somewhat less pressured than when I was attending the Catholic school system. I finally had the opportunity to play soccer in our large playground area behind our home with my new friends that I was growing up with. The coursework, like I said before, was very demanding and the homework was sometimes overwhelming. The courses that gave me the most difficulties were the Italian language, especially the essay portion, together with Algebra. During this year, my father decided to see if he could obtain a technical school certificate just to help him in his job advancements, since everything was getting more technically demanding. He ordered a full course of technical books, which also covered Algebra through Trigonometry. This was those early in-home curricula, or correspondence schools, that when you completed them, you send in all the tests taken and the company would issue some kind of technical school certificate. Today, we call these remote learning or online learning, but there were no computers in those days. My father would need to send all the tests back to the school and if it met their passing criteria, that certificate of achievement would be on its way. I remember counting more than 100 very thin booklets each one of them teaching different aspects of each course with a test to take at the end of each booklet. My father started studying and reading these mini books and initially he did put some effort into them, but I think it was short lived due to his work and overwhelming family obligations. Unfortunately, he was not able to finish this course and did not get that technical certificate. These books, though, helped me at times with my schoolwork and homework, especially since they explained the basics of Algebra in more layman terms. What really impressed me was the more advanced subjects that were covered as you went along to subsequent courses. These technical resources really enlightened me on what I was going to be up against in the coming years.

The economy in Italy also hit some low points that year (1966). Inflation was going up but the paychecks were not. My father had been asking for a raise every so often from the company during all the past years. Every time he asked, he was told that it was unlikely since sales and expenses at the shipyard were under pressure or below projections. As an example, he would ask for a $25.00 monthly raise and he would be lucky to maybe get $5.00 instead, hardly keeping up with inflation. I think he became a little discouraged with his job and that was reflected in his way of thinking that changed during those years.

Getting back to my first year in pre-high school, the scholastic end of the year was fast approaching, and exams would soon start. The exams given for each of the courses included both a written and oral portion. The written part was not too hard to take but the oral exams were very demanding. It usually consisted of three or four professors sitting behind a large rectangular desk just like a large bench of judges. These professors, including your own, all taught the same subject during different periods of the day and with different students. A list of all of the students' names was posted on the school's bulletin board along with the day and time that the student was scheduled to take their exam.

The list included maybe fifty students for each daily session of exams. Just to get a feel of what this exam was like, let me give you an example. Let's take the European history exam. You would first wait and sit in this large exam room together with all the other students scheduled for that day's session. Your name is called at some point by the one of the professors. You would approach the slightly raised bench and sit at a desk situated in front of them. You could not bring any notes or textbooks with you. The professors would have your class history textbook in front of them, possibly with a bookmark at a particular section that they wanted to test you on. Each professor would take turns questioning you. The first thing that one of the professors would say is, "Is this the textbook that your class has used?" He would then hold it up so that you could recognize it. The reason for this was that the history curriculum had two or three books selected as the class textbook. Each professor had their own preference as to which book they preferred to teach their class with. The Italian National Committee on Education approved all of the textbooks for each school year. Some textbooks could be used for two years since they covered a large historic period, so you can imagine how voluminous and how expensive some of them were.

Getting back to the oral test, they would begin, "Signor Galliani, I am turning the book to a chapter that covers a time before Christ was born. I would like you to tell us about Alexander the Great. Can you please give us details when he lived, his family background, his accomplishments, why he was called 'The Great' and anything else that you can contribute?" Hence, everything was from your memory and recollections. If you studied and retained information on Alexander the Great, you were golden. You are half-scared to death just to be in front of these professors, plus the other students waiting for their turn were also listening to your answers, but their question would not be the same. You are just eleven years old. How would you like to be exposed to this kind of school testing? What do you say if you do not know or recall any of these facts for that particular history question? This is one of those times in your life that you begin to learn how to interact with the real world and life in general. Did you study the history book? Are you smart enough to answer that question? Maybe you just want to be honest and say "I am sorry, I do not recall those facts." The questioning would then proceed to the next professor until all three or four of them have asked you their own questions. You would be graded by each one of the professors and their summary score posted on same the board by the end of the week once all the students were tested. This would go on for about two weeks until you were orally tested on all your core subjects taken during that school year. The grading system at the time ranged from 1 to 10. A five was a passing grade in some subjects, but an actual passing score was more often a six. To make things even worse, they would use the plus or minus sign with each grade and sometimes that made the difference. The grade of nine or ten was rarely given; eight would be an incredible achievement. If you failed to get a passing grade in any of the subjects, you were assigned to retake the tests at the end of August. This meant that your summer vacation was essentially destroyed. The whole summer would be wasted studying in order to pass the failed courses to be promoted to the next grade.

Unfortunately, I didn't pass some of my 6th grade exams in English and Latin. My parents were disappointed with my results and had to make some financial sacrifices that summer. They hired a tutor for the months of June and July to help me pass the second testing opportunity. Through their acquaintances, they were able to secure a young college student who was smart and able to help me prepare for the August tests instead of a more expensive seasoned professor working during his school vacation. These sharp and smart college students would charge a lesser fee, and they would also work out of their parents' home, all in all a very good option. My parents could afford their reduced fees, but I am sure that they would have rather used that money for other summer activities if I just passed all the courses in May and was promoted. To this day, I totally regret my failure to pass those subjects that year. It would have spared everyone the added burden and grief, not to mention missing many summer beach days. During that summer I had to tell my friends many times, that "I can't come to the beach with you guys today, I have tutoring lessons. I will see you tonight." Then, when I saw them at night, I felt even worse because they would tell me "You should have seen all the beautiful girls at the beach today!"

During that summer of 1966, something else happened that was much more significant than my scholastic failures. My father made the decision that we would apply to immigrate to the United States. This event would change our family's life and destiny. To this day, I cannot think for sure what really triggered the decision that my father made. I don't recall if there was some specific event or a series of events that spawned my father to make that decision. I feel that this was one of the questions that only my father could have answered. I had almost thirty plus years of my adult life at my disposal to ask him this question, but I never did. When my father passed away in late 2004, he took that answer with him to the grave. The question that I should have asked him was and still is "Why did you, Papa, decide to immigrate to America?" I have tried to get second-hand answers from the elders and the surviving members of my family during my research in writing of this book. I asked this question first to my mother and then to her two sisters living in Italy that had some firsthand accounts of those days. None of their answers really struck a core in me as being my father's real reason. But maybe there is no real answer, it may be something that ferments in you and one day it finally, for some reason or no reason at, all boils over. For my mother when I asked her, she brushed it off saying that my father was a man that liked to change and move around to find new opportunities. My mother's sisters in Italy told me a different story from their perspective. They speculated that my father's decision was based on evaluating my future and that of my siblings versus our opportunities in Italy. He always thought that the next generation required new opportunities and a better environment than that which he grew up in. In those times, Italy's economy was not in great shape and many people struggled to get ahead. Jobs were also scarce, and many people had to peddle politicians and pay them for a secure lifetime job. The political incorrectness and mentality was not something that he cared to see or be involved with. In Italy, who you knew meant more than what you knew. My father was a staunch believer that individuals had to prove themselves with their qualifications and hard work, not politics. I guess he was an early adopter of the so-called "merit system" and how it should be applied to modern day American immigration policy. With this thinking, he was able to give a lot of consideration to his children's future while living in Italy. He recognized that it was not a miracle to be well respected at his job, it took a lot of perseverance, hard work and sacrifices to be so accepted and rewarded by his employer. The probability of us achieving our goals and being compensated or exceling in Italy was somewhat limited in his thinking. His past experiences with the Americans at the Air Force base in Tripoli probably also played some kind of role with his final decision. Notwithstanding my mother's very persistent disagreements for taking this monumental step, which still resonates in her recollection even today in her 80s, my father decided in late 1966 to file an application with the American embassy in Palermo, the capital of Sicily, to be considered to immigrate to the United States of America.

What kind of direct connection did my father have with America? How did this really become a relevant option? To bring this into perspective, since the 1950s, my father had kept an open line of communication via mail with my mother's first cousins that were living in Boston, Massachusetts. They emigrated from Tripoli a few years before we also left for Messina, Italy. I remember that in the early 1960s my great uncle, who lived in northern Italy, visited his sons and daughter in Boston every few years and also came to see us in Messina two times. He told my father about his sons, that shortly thereafter they arrived in the US, they opened a machine shop business near Boston. He also told my father that his sons' business "The machine shop" was really thriving in Boston and they had a great future in front of them. I guess this was something that really struck a nerve with my father and must have been on his mind after that. I believe that the opportunity of personal and financial achievements possible in the United States played an important role in his decision process. These thoughts became even more evident during some difficult financial times in Messina. He considered the notion that if I would have the same opportunities in America that I got here in Messina, I could achieve a lot more there and be handsomely rewarded.

But now you may wonder, how and when did our family immigration cycle start? How did it happen that my mother's cousins were able to come to America? We need to go back again in time to my grandfather, Vincenzo. I spoke about him extensively in the 'Out of Africa' section. During that period, my grandfather was already in his 50s, but I never mentioned what he did or where he went, many years before he got married. This is where I want to take you briefly to describe his whereabouts in the early part of the 19th century. I did not want to cover that in the first part of the book because 'Out of Africa' was intended to strictly describe our family life in Libya. We can now come to a full circle in understanding my family's immigration plight.

When he was a young single man, maybe in his early twenties, my grandfather decided to follow his older brother, Paulo, who immigrated to America in 1909 and settled in California. The Immigration Act, enacted in 1882, established a 50-cent tax to enter the United States, to be paid by each immigrant upon entry. It was not until the Immigration Act of 1924, also known as the Johnson-Reed Act, that quotas and other regulations were established to limit immigration from all countries. Based on the earlier Immigration Act, my grandfather Vincenzo arrived in 1919 at Ellis Island, paid his 50-cent tax and was admitted to the U.S. Ellis Island records uncovered during my research for this book revealed the exact date and the ship that verifies my grandfather's entry into the United States. Immigration records at Ellis Island showed that he wrote down that he had a brother that lived in California. My grandfather did not join Paulo in California, but ended up going to Boston where he found work in a bakery, in a location now called East Boston. His accounts of his Massachusetts stay to my mother and her sisters, his three daughters correlated with this story. He worked in a bakery and his job would start very early each morning, usually before 4:00 AM. The bakery would open to the public at 6:00 AM. The first customers would arrive before going to work to buy my grandfather's freshly baked bread for their daily meal. Unfortunately, my grandfather did not like this American experience, and after working for a few years he decided to return to his home country several years before the 1929 depression. But during his tenure in the U.S., he facilitated the immigration of three of his sisters and two of his brothers. When he left America, he did not go back to Italy, but instead went to Libya where one of his remaining brothers had started a small business in Tripoli. I guess you can safely say that my grandfather, Vincenzo, was pretty much the family patriarch and planted the roots of my family's destiny and final immigration to America, long before he passed.

How my mother's first cousins ended up in Boston is also significant. The two very young sisters that Vincenzo helped to settle in Boston in the late 1920s worked hard during their stay in the U.S. They eventually opened an Italian cold cuts sub shop in the suburbs of Boston in the late 1940s after World War II. As we all recall, that time period was also known as the Baby Boom and the American economy was firing on all cylinders. These sisters and their husbands expanded the food store due to overwhelming demand for their services, which called for additional help. One of the sisters recalled their young nephews living in Tripoli. They reached out to the boys' father

'Ciccio', who shortly before had become a widow due to his wife contracting cancer. They explained to him that they would take care of his kids, now teenagers, and that they would live and work with them at their Food Market. The adults agreed that it would be best for them if they could join their aunts in America. Since they were direct blood relatives, the sisters were able to sponsor their nephews to come to America, all according to those days' immigration laws.

My father's application for immigration to the United States listed our cousins living in Boston for more than ten years as the guarantors. The reader may ask by now what were the immigration laws in the 1960s? From my research, the following law was passed in 1965. The Immigration and Naturalization Act of 1965, also known as the Hart-Celler Act, abolished an earlier quota system based on national origin and established a new immigration policy based on reuniting immigrant families and attracting skilled labor to the United States. From this act, we can gather that the United States government wanted families living in different parts of the world to be reunited. It also introduced the factor that if you were a skilled worker, you would be prioritized. My father, from his point of view together with what you have read so far, was a man that waited for no train to pass. He would find it and go there to jump on it. There was no waiting for him. He would press with resiliency and endurance until he achieved his goals. This was the story of his life as you can confirm from many passages in this book. In order to expedite the entry to the U.S., he contacted one of the cousins. He had learned from their father's visit to our home that they now owned their own business, a "Machine Shop." They might have a business relationship with a company that was in search of a skilled diesel mechanic.

Our family qualified for the first part of the Hart-Celler Act because we showed intent to be reunited with direct blood relatives. The second part of this law provided expedited incentive such as shorter processing times in order to attract skilled labor to the United States. If our cousins could find a company that would also sponsor my father because of their work needs, then the process could be expedited. The wait for an immigration approval and green card was not known to us. There was no Internet and everything moved by postal mail. It could take one, two, or three years or it may get lost altogether in political bureaucracy and the process would reset and all had to be reaffirmed. My father's luck came shortly after he filed his initial immigration application. My mother's cousins, which by the way I called them uncles for respect, were able to find a sponsor for my father. They learned that one of their machine shop clients, a trucking company, was in search of an experienced diesel mechanic to maintain their fleet of trucks. They approached the owner and presented to them my father's skillset and experience. They mentioned that my father had already filed papers with the American embassy in Italy to immigrate to America. My father's skills were above the owner's needs but he agreed to sponsor him and to hire him to work at his trucking company if he was granted entry to the United States. There was one little problem with the immigration law which was in the fine print of the sponsorship of a foreign worker. The Immigration Act made it mandatory that the sponsor satisfy some preconditions. The most important requirement was that the job application had to be advertised first in one of that major city's newspapers for two weeks, clearly describing all the qualifications and experience needed. Only if no other American citizen was found to satisfy the employer needs could the employer initiate the sponsorship documents for this alien with the immigration department. The immigration services in Boston required that all pre-requisite documents were to be filed by the employer and, if approved, then they would bind the additional work sponsorship contract to my father's immigration papers at the American embassy in Italy. Things looked up by the end of 1966. All we had to do now was wait and see if and when an acceptance letter would arrive from the American embassy to our Messina home.

I was now attending 7th grade since I was finally promoted by passing the August exams. As I divulged in starting this new school year, academics became not the only issue during that time period. I recall that the atmosphere in our household had somehow changed from that of the previous year. My mother was not fully onboard with my father's decision to leave Italy if we were granted permission to immigrate and that impacted my school work. My studying habits were changed due to their bickering over this decision. Something had disrupted the normal course of everyday life when my father finalized the immigration papers and sent them all to the American embassy. Everyone was quite tense and I think there was a real fear of what was going to happen. I can definitely say today that my mother was always a pessimist and my father was always an optimist. When it came to emigrating, once again, my mother always feared the worst and she had good reasons. Our last immigration from Tripoli was not a positive experience for everyone and she feared that this one would be even worse. I can recall her saying to him "Why do you want to leave behind what we have now finally accomplished here and give it all away again for an unknown future?" There was a lot of back and forth bickering between them during this time frame that we were waiting for a response from the United States embassy. I remember that sometimes late at night they would start arguing mainly about my father's stubbornness. My mother, a devoted wife from the very beginning, endured the many sacrifices that we encountered from the very beginning of our arrival in Italy from Libya. She was not wrong in her way of thinking. For his part, my father wanted less pressure, more financial reward, and to be fully recognized for his accomplishments. It seemed that he was not happy with his job at the shipyard anymore. My father would tell her of some events that he had to endure because incompetent people performed their work incorrectly and he had to cover for them. There was too much class distinction that existed at work. I witnessed this firsthand myself. You see my father was not shy in bringing me to the shipyard from time to time and on that wonderful trip out to sea.

I must have been twelve years old during one of those shipyard visits. I recall distinctly the first thing that I noticed while walking in the large hangers, was that some workers were wearing dark blue technician coveralls and some were wearing white coveralls. My father always wore the dark blue, all-in-one jumpsuit, popular of those days. Remember the TV series "Happy Days?" Do you recall seeing Fonzie working on his motorcycle? He was always seen wearing his mechanic jumpsuit. That was my father, and he also looked a little bit like Fonzie then. I asked him, "Can you tell me the difference between you and the employees wearing the lighter color clothes?" He would comment, "See, I and all the others wearing the dark blue clothing, we get dirty sometimes because we actually have to assemble the engines or make repairs. Thus, an almost white working suit would get dirty very quickly here. The one wearing the white coveralls, their job is to evaluate the repairs and to supervise our work especially during any new engine's final assembly. These are the people that have school degrees, they know the engines from a paper perspective." But he said to me that some of them could not even hold a mechanical tool correctly if one was handed to them. He also explained that their supervisory responsibility was to make sure that all the work was done in accordance with pre-described procedures and mechanical specification. "These so-called engineers sometimes make our work harder than it should be, by interrupting the flow of work by asking to see that things were done correctly. In several instances, they would ask my team to take apart work that was already completed even after I told them that I already had double checked it. It didn't happen very often but when it did it was not a great feeling for me. This put a lot of strain on our team relationship, because they essentially put our work schedule back and someone, like me, had to make up for that lost time." He was right, I noticed that they all walked around with papers or folders in their hands. "The documents in their hands would be handed to higher management that showed that they approved and inspected our work. So, they really never got their hands or coveralls dirty since they really never came in contact with the engine or any of the oily parts." My father understood this possible intellectual disparity but he could not comprehend the large salary disparity.

He became more vocal with his complaints about his job with my mother. I remember him saying, "I am working so hard, but I am not really being compensated for what I produce. Every time there was some kind of event or mishap at the shipyard, I have to scramble to make it right. I have to cover sometimes for others' mistakes and rectify them myself." He would refer to the person that performed the faulty work by saying in Sicilian Italian "Quella testa di gesso" translated to "That individual has a gypsum head," a saying that that individual was incompetent. They possessed a degree, but they knew nothing when it came to doing things hands on. All of the large mechanical drawings were done by hand and a slide rule. This was his frustration, especially the large salary disparity. These and other things really changed his attitude from that of previous years. Now a mature man in the mid-thirties, the real-life pressures and consciousness started to get the better of him. My mother, many times, would try to calm him down and say "Don't worry. You see? Everything will get resolved soon." He would counter "Yes, I want to leave this country if I get the opportunity. Can you imagine your kids if they grow up and experience what I have? I don't want them to endure this same kind of aggravation and daily contests to prove themselves, I am not sure I can stand or allow that to happen."

Finally, the year 1967 came and, like they say, the New Year brought new resolutions and expectations. For my part, I was again not performing well in school. This time it was English and Algebra II. I was spending some afternoons studying at my friend's home, trying to catch up with my schoolwork. My brother and sister were getting even noisier than the previous year, and it was too hard to concentrate on my studies at home. I guess the apartment was also getting too small for all five of us. Maybe my father had sensed this and that he would soon have to move to a bigger home, but he probably thought that on his current salary it would be an uphill battle. Maybe he felt trapped by the current circumstances and events. He probably thought that he would never be able to achieve financial goals that would take care of the family especially now that the kids were growing up. More expenses would be in the forefront and his salary was not keeping up with our upcoming needs.

As the year 1967 moved along, everyone was on edge. Spring came and no word from the American consulate on our immigration application. It was now over nine months. For my part, I was trying to do the best I could in the 7th grade, but it looked like those difficult subjects were getting the best of me. The family household was at a standstill, my mother, father and I, the oldest sibling of the house, did not ask any questions or engage in any conversations that would start an argument. The weight of our pending American immigration application reply was always on everyone's mind. It was like living at the edge of a mountain looking down but never seeing the green pastures below, because there was always a dense fog below. Then, finally, a letter came from the American consulate in Palermo. I believe this was in May of 1967. I distinctly recall that my mother did not open that letter with the American Embassy seal. She placed it standing up on the dining table leaning against the empty crystal center vase. The letter was addressed to my father, and she said that he would open it when he came home. When my father finally arrived around 6:00 PM, we greeted him like every other day. But the home felt to me like all of the oxygen had been taken out. I had a feeling that something important would transpire on that day. I would be proven right. That day marked the beginning of a lifetime event that would change everyone's destiny.

I want to take a moment in my recollection of that day to let the reader know one of the great aspects of my upbringing during the years that I lived in Italy. My mother taught all of us kids from a very young age one basic respectful behavior in greeting our father when he would come in the door from his daily work. When my father entered the door of our home from work and walked into our house, no matter what we were doing, we would leave everything and go hug and kiss my father. This was our way, according to the Old Italian culture, to acknowledge my father's sacrifices after a full day at his job. It also recognized that the leader of the family had come back home safe and sound on that day. It showed that we were glad that he was back home and that we loved him. I must say that after our hugs, my mother would also go and share an affectionate kiss or embrace depending on her disposition. My father really enjoyed this, and I think it gave him a sense of satisfaction and self-accomplishment. This gesture also intended to let him know that his workday was over, and should he have had a bad day at work, he was now safe with his family that loved him. This aspect of my upbringing as it is related to my father, and please don't ask me why and how, slowly faded away throughout the years as we grew older but it stopped when we became part of the American environment.

The oversized white envelope was waiting for him smack in the middle of the dining table. It stood out like a sore thumb. I don't recall any other occasion when a piece of mail was ever distinctively placed there. I vividly remember my father approaching the table after our daily welcome, putting his empty lunch box on one of the chairs and reaching out to pick up this envelope. He read the front and quickly understood that it was an important communication from the American Embassy. He put it back down and went to wash his hands and freshen up. He would also change his work clothes like he did any other day. He walked back to the table and opened the envelope very slowly and carefully, making sure that he didn't damage any of the contents inside. He sat down on the chair, pulled the papers out of the envelope and started to read the first page. There was a silence in the house. You could have heard a pin drop. My mother was at the stove about ten feet away from the kitchen table. She was waiting for the water to boil so that she could put the pasta in to cook. I think my father must have read it at least two times because it took him almost ten minutes before he neatly put it back in the envelope. My mother looked like she wasn't too interested because she probably sensed that something was going to change dramatically again and she had already experienced this. My mother was ready for the meal and she brought it to the table where we all took our places. As we sat down, and as my mother was distributing the pasta to all of our dishes, my father conveyed the news contained in the letter. He said that our application for immigration to the United States was accepted. The letter asked us to go to the consulate on a particular date approximately thirty days from now with all our medical documents that were requested of us. He explained that everyone in our family needed to show that we were fully vaccinated and that a short physical examination would be done at the Consulate by an American doctor. Pending verification of everyone's health status together with the other previously filed papers, a decision would be made after this visit if the Embassy would grant everyone a Green Card for immigration to the United States of America. There was a deadening sound again in the room. Nothing was said and we all started to eat dinner. I understood what that letter meant, being the eldest child. My siblings ate their food like nothing happened; they just wanted to leave the table and go play with their toys.

My mother did not say anything during dinner that I can recall, but her face did not show much happiness.

I also recall that in May 1967, the school notified me that I failed to achieve a passing grade in two of my classes again that year. Of all subjects it was the foreign language "English" and the usual math course, but this time it was "Geometry 2" which is actually "Trigonometry" by American standards. After the school year ended for both me and my sister, who was now attending third grade, the family drove to the American embassy in Palermo sometime in June 1967 to keep that appointment, pass the physical exams, and sign the necessary paperwork. If everything was in order with the current American laws and health requirements, an alien residency Green Card would be issued to each of us shortly thereafter, so that everyone could enter the United States as a legal permanent alien. I still think about that two-hour plus trip in our car from Messina to Palermo where the U.S. Consulate was located. It seemed to me that we were going on a vacation. We never drove that far from the city before. When we arrived, we walked into this big white brick building with a big symbol, an Eagle emblem, and the words "USA Consulate General" on the front door. There were not many people in the waiting room, which differed from the crowded and noisy Italian institutions. The waiting room was bright, clean, and neat and everyone there was busy doing their job. They were all speaking mostly English, but sometimes I would hear a few Italian words. There was a sense of tranquility, even if my parents looked quite nervous. I guess I got my first taste of the American way of doing business. It was very organized and everyone seemed to know their work responsibilities. Everyone had a pile of folders on their desks, some thin but others substantially thick. After a brief wait, our last name was called and we were asked in Italian to approach that front desk. My father carried and delivered all of our identification papers including the other ones requested by the consulate in their letter. After we were checked in, all of us were moved to a different room, where I believe a doctor that also spoke some Italian reviewed our health records. Some important questions were asked to my parents about us, the children's health, and also about theirs. Everyone passed the required immunization schedule except for my five-year-old brother, Vincenzo. He was found deficient of a key vaccination in order to abide by the health rules of the United States. Wow! America actually had regulations in their immigration laws in those years. Did they vanish now? Or are they just being ignored? Are they no longer important to the health of their current citizens? My readers can decide on that aspect of the old immigration standards.

I don't recall if Vincenzo received that vaccination there or if my mother took him to our family doctor at home and sent the document back. In any case, the Embassy needed that done and it was done. To expand on this event, please be forewarned, if you should ever encounter my brother Vincenzo, "Vinny," today. He stands about 5'11" tall and 220lbs, a spitting image of the actor Steven Seagal with a pulled back pony tail and boots. You may not want to bring up any immigration issues or discuss the above vaccine story with him in order for him to join us in the American dream. You will get an earful from him on what he had to go through to get it done at a very young age in order to make it to America. Additionally, if you get him peeved, he will roll up his sleeve and show you the scar on his large left bicep that was left from that vaccination. He may not be happy to have that scar, but he is proud of having it. His arm is proof of what it took for him to receive his Green Card in order to be allowed to come to America. How does that fare with the many aliens that pretty much come in as tourists and decide to remain here, or the individuals that just walk into our great country and ask to be admitted just because they are here? Are they fully immunized and have they received a physical exam? He will tell you not to ask any more questions or else you will get yourself in trouble.

Within thirty days of our medical visit, we received a letter from the embassy at our home that said "Congratulations! You have been accepted for legal entry to the United States of America. Please bring with you all the attached certified documents together with the enclosed Green Alien cards for each family member. These will be required by the American immigration service at your port of entry when you arrive in USA." There was a sober silence again in our house as my parents realized that they now were given legal immigration status in the U.S. All we had to do now was pack everything up and be on our way to the United States of America anytime we wanted. The Green Alien card was good for five years at which point you could renew it and if you lived in the U.S. for that time you could apply for American citizenship.

The days and weeks following this were very hectic. It was now late June and I was again being tutored to pass seventh grade exams since I again failed the previously mentioned subjects in order to be promoted to the 8th grade which was to be the final grade in the Italian school system before high school. That summer was very disruptive to all of us while my father was making arrangements to leave Italy. But, it would take months to put everything in order with everyone. Just as importantly for my father was how to notify his current job that he would be leaving. Our lives would never be the same ever again. What awaited us was an unknown fate, but we trusted our father's decision for better or for worse. My mother was never 100% on board with the whole idea of leaving Italy for good. But when my father told her about his meeting with the management at the shipyard in order to let them know that he would be resigning because he was leaving for the U.S., things got a little more difficult and overheated at home. My mother and my father argued back and forth about this event and what transpired in that meeting with the management at the shipyard. The following is my innocent account of what transpired in the following days and possibly weeks.

The story goes this way, according to my mother: that after my father gave management his resignation notice, one of the owners of the Rodriquez Shipyard asked him to make an appointment because he wanted to talk in private with him. This gentleman was one of the principals and was directly related to the original founder of the Rodriquez Company. You will get to know him better in the final portion of this book when we all get a dose of what the "Circle of Life" is all about. For now, I would just like you to know a little bit about him. The most important thing was that he always recognized my father's talent throughout all of the years that he worked at his shipyard. He also was the one that recommended my father as the most qualified mechanic to send on those Egyptian trips to help in the delivery of the newly purchased hydrofoils. Additionally, he made sure that during his management tenure, my father was always kept up to date with the latest technical training. My understanding is that he saw him as an invaluable asset to the whole company. When they finally met face to face, he said that he was very saddened and disappointed that my father made the decision to leave his company and immigrate to the United States. He respectfully asked if my father would reconsider his decision while he consulted with all the other members of the management team. He asked my father if they could meet again in a few days to pick up the conversation. My father was very receptive and respectful of his boss' request and accepted this follow up meeting. It is worth mentioning here from my research, that this individual was also responsible for those bonuses that my father would receive from time to time in his paycheck.

What follows in this book may be a little disconcerting for some of our readers, but please keep an open mind. Sometimes life is full of twists and turns, most of them unexpected. It all happened late in the summer of 1967, and when those decisions were made they became part of my family history. Money was not the only thing important to my father. His prestige and pride together with his strong ethics sometimes got the best of him. Life sometimes changes in the blink of an eye and there is no time for looking or going back. Maybe down the line and many years from now you might say "Wow, I should have been a little more conscientious and thorough with my decision." But my father was not someone that would look back or could be swayed very easily once he made up his mind.

The story goes this way, according to my mother. Mr. Rodriquez, during the follow-up meeting, offered my father a great opportunity to rethink his decision, remain in Italy, and play a prominent part in his company's future. "After much consultation with my management team," Mr. Rodriquez said, "I want you to know that we all have recognized that you, 'Giorgio,' play a central role here at our company. You have been recognized by the mechanical engineering team as an integral part of our shipbuilding company. Your work and dedication also have not gone unnoticed by all of us in the management team. I want you to know that we respect your decision to leave the company, but we want to give you one last opportunity to rethink your decision. We would like to put on the table an opportunity to remain here and become part of our company's growth and future. Our company is willing to offer you a substantial promotion and a new management position in the city of Naples where we are planning to open a new satellite office complex. You, Mr. Galliani, will be given a key leadership position at this new location and, based on what we have seen in the past, we believe that you will play a relevant role for any of our future ventures in Italy. Your technical expertise and experience from all the years working at the shipyard makes you instrumental in supporting the technical and mechanical aspects of our future sales. To compensate you in this newly created position, we are willing to double your monthly salary. In addition, we would like to pay for all the expenses for moving your family to Naples and also help you in finding a new home with the resources that we have in that city. We cherish your work and dedication, having said this, we would like you to reconsider your immigration plans and stay with our company as the technical manager at this new Rodriquez location in Naples. We would like you to take all the time you need, to discuss this with your wife and family. PLEASE come back to us after fully considering this offer and your final decision on this matter. We are planning this move in the next few months and we would like to find out if you will be part of this initial project with our company."

I can only tell you that at twelve years old, this was not a very happy time for me witnessing this event and also being there when the final decision was made. My father, on that particular day after that meeting, was home much earlier than usual. He sat at the table while my mother was preparing dinner for that night. He asked my mother to leave the food simmering on the stove and to listen to what had happened during his meeting at work with management. For my part, I was just faking that I was reading a book and not paying much attention, but I was all ears. He presented the details of that job offer that was put on the table for him with my mother. I recall listening to their conversation, while I kept faking my reading. I could hear some of the key points, especially when my mother would raise her voice slightly in order to get her point across. The basic issue that my mother correctly made to my father was that of the large salary increase. It was something that did not happen every day, it was a once in a lifetime event. The other was that his "new work position as a technical manager meant that getting your hands dirty would be a thing of the past. You will oversee and delegate to other mechanics and put your skills to work only when needed." I also want my readers to understand that with these financial terms, our family would have been able to afford a much bigger home for our growing family. My mother also added that "we would not have to struggle that much anymore to make ends meet and that your kids would have a new life in that new city." Regrettably, my father was not on the same page with her. He pointed out to her, "How many times have I asked the company for a small raise in the last several years to only receive a small percentage of what I asked for or none at all? I do not trust them," he said, "They have not been there when I really needed them to come to my aid. I understand that from time to time, I would receive a little extra in my paycheck but that was due to the kindness of one person - way too little and much too late. Now that they are faced with my departure they are offering me the world. What do they think, that I am a child? They are now throwing a bunch of candy at me like I am a little boy so I can stay put? Why have they not been forthcoming when it really counted! I have no faith there, plus the new job will require a lot of long days with long hours." Notwithstanding my father's observations, my mother begged him to reconsider. She would say "Think about your kids, they will grow up in a better environment and have new opportunities. We can finally move out of this small apartment and live in a better place." My father countered to my mother by saying, "In America, I already have a job contract and we can make a fresh start there. Maybe I can start my own business just like your cousins." My mother said, "We don't know what we are going to find there, I don't speak the English language, and we would again start all over like we did when we came to Italy from Libya. My father said, "Everyone that I know has done well in America, your cousins own their own business, they own their home, and they live a good life from what we can gather. We have been here for almost nine years. We still do not own our apartment. It is small and the kids are growing up fast. If we were in the United States for these last nine years, I bet we would have been a lot better off maybe just like your cousins or more." My mother said, "Giorgio, remember, 'not all that glitters is gold.'" My father said, "I really made up my mind. I have put so much in this immigration plan and now is time to move on, and I want to go there." My mother said, "Okay! I will always back your decision! Can I just ask you to at least go to America alone, see it for yourself while we wait for you here? Go there and see if everything is what we all expect it to be, your new job in America, the city, and all that is needed for us to live a new comfortable life there. Me and the children, we will come there after a couple of months or when you feel that all is set." My father would have none of that. Again, he said "Where I go everyone follows, we are a family that moves together." I guess we can witness my father's real Italian character coming out. I remember my mother weeping and struggling with his attitude. She could not convince him to reconsider the offer or at least go to America without all of us initially. I think that night and many that followed were not a very pleasant time. A lot of grief was expressed, especially by my mother, which continued for days thereafter.

I guess when everything was finally settled, my father met again with Mr. Rodriquez and told him that he was committed to leave. He also reiterated to him, "Why are you offering this financial incentive now? If you only had given me that raise when I asked so many times, I would have never contemplated leaving Italy." My father, much later in our life told me an interesting part of their last conversation. He recalled what Mr. Rodriquez voiced to him during their last meeting, "Giorgio, I want you to know as you are very aware, and I have travelled all around the world. I have been to the United States many times, let me just tell you the streets are not paved or covered with gold as many in Italy believe. You work really hard there, you may be able to make a good living there, but it is not a "Walk in The Park" and it is not for the fainthearted. I am saddened that you have decided to leave us, but I wish the best and much fortune in the United States." He also ended by telling him, "Should you need any help in the U.S., please let me know, I have many friends that live there."

This was my father's last life changing decision and even if my mother did not agree with it, we all packed up and went along. I am not stating that my father made the wrong decision then, but it definitely was NOT "A walk in the park" as you will see later in this book. We are all doing well today, thriving and living a bit of the American dream. All I am saying is that our decision is not at all a reflection of what the average American immigrant came here for. We did not come from the farmland, and we were not really struggling to make a living in the homeland. We did experience some hardship but not nearly as much as many immigrant families that came to America from Italy or any other country for that manner. Many of them were really exposed to and endured much suffering in their life before they immigrated to America.

In Italy, we were living in a fairly modern city. We owned a car. We had running hot water. We had a washing machine, and a fairly new apartment. It was very small, but clean. Notwithstanding on how limited those resources appear today, we were blessed during our life in Messina. We just had to watch every penny we spent in order to make ends meet with my father's salary. The politics were also impelling; they played a large role in everyday Italian life. It was, again, very evident to my father, that what made many things go around in Italy was not "What you know, but who you know." My father felt that we, the kids, would struggle like him in our future in Italy, especially if we didn't know someone that would give us a push. This consideration that he made, that his children would be better off in America than Italy, together with a better educational opportunity, must have sealed his decision.

It was decided that we would leave Italy around mid-October on an ocean liner. The main reasons behind this approach was that a ship gave us the option to take most of our belongings with us. We did not have a lot, but what we had was exquisite items like handmade house linens and table cloths. We also had silverware and very unique house decorations purchased by my father during his trips outside of Italy. My mother also wanted to make sure that no gifts from her wedding in Libya were left behind. The ship gave us the option to bring with us large crates or "bauli" as they call them in Italian. Bauli are large, nicely finished wooden boxes measuring as much as five feet long by three plus feet deep. We purchased three of these in order to have enough space for all the items that my parents wanted to bring to America. These crates would travel with us on the ship and then be transported to our final destination via truck after we arrived to our final destination.

My Aunt Anna's father in-law during that period was the Port Master in Messina. He facilitated most of our logistics and was also able to obtain some preferential treatment for us on that ship, bound for New York. My father gathered whatever money he had saved, including that from the sale of his car and other house furniture that was no longer needed. This was not much - maybe $2,500.00 or so - including the bank savings that would help us to get us started in America. One positive fact about our departure was that we were able to keep and rent out the government owned apartment. We would still be obligated to pay the monthly fee to the government which would be mostly covered by the rent. That was really neat. It meant that we still had a home to go back to if things really turned out badly. But nobody ever thought that it would happen. I knew in my heart that we would never come back or live in that home again. I should have started eighth grade in September, but since my father decided to leave on October 20th of 1967 to be exact, I did not go to school in Italy when it opened that year in the fall. There was just too much going on and no real purpose for going to school for a little more than a month.

I can still remember the day that we left Messina on that beautiful ocean liner. It reminds me today of that old TV show "The Love Boat." But there was no love there, just a lot of hope. My mother's sisters and their families came to the city port to wish us luck and say their last goodbye. We were accompanied onboard the ship by my aunt's father in-law just to make us feel more secure and in good hands. Due to his important role as an authority at the Port of Messina, he was allowed to come on board with us briefly. He spoke personally to the ship's captain and asked him to make sure that we were taken care of during our trip to America. Talking about knowing people! Just one more example of Italy's political way of life. The ocean liner that we boarded was named the TSS Olympia. It was one of three ships that were part of a Greek owned company. The ship was built as the TSS Olympia in Glasgow, Scotland in 1953. She was the first and only ship ever to be built for the Greek Line, as well as being the largest built for Greek interests at the time. Olympia was designed to operate with regular transatlantic voyages, between Piraeus and New York, stopping in Italy and other ports on the way to New York. The ship was also used as a seasonal cruise ship when not travelling across the ocean.

Olympia was built to accommodate a total of 1,356 passengers, most of these travelling in Tourist Class, carrying only a small number in First Class. She had a number of interchangeable cabins for 146 passengers. The reason she was built as a predominantly Tourist class ship was in response to a demand for cheaper travel during the post-war years. Olympia had eight passenger decks: Sports (Boat) Deck, Sun Deck, Promenade Deck, Upper Deck, Main Deck, A Deck, B Deck, and C Deck.

The Olympia. The ship that took us across the ocean to America.

I still recall vividly as the ship slowly pulled away. Everyone was by the ship rail facing the port dock. All of the passengers' relatives were gathered to say their last goodbyes to their beloved ones. At my age, I did not realize what was actually happening. I was too young to perceive or understand the impact of that day. Unfortunately, my parents were fully aware of that. My mother was crying as she waved to her sisters below. Our approximate seven-day trip was now underway. It also marks the abrupt ending of our Italian life which concludes the end of this second part of my book. I consider this the last "Out of Italy" paragraph since having left Messina, the city that had been our home for almost ten years, we were now truly separated from the Italian homeland.

The voyage on this ship to America, I consider it part of my third and final portion of this book. This is the beginning of the "Coming to America" final chapter of my family's trek. Hopefully I was able to bring some colorful history for everyone to enjoy and hopefully you learned a little bit about the fiber of my family in the 1960s and my childhood. The destiny of some people is sometimes entrenched with the views and decisions of strong-minded ones with a vision for a better future. As we embark on this final journey, everything from this point on will mark for us for the second time a new beginning.

COMING TO AMERICA

Our ocean liner moved away toward the Mediterranean Sea. The ship was scheduled to make two stops before crossing the Atlantic Ocean. The first stop was in the Port of Genoa on the northern coast of Italy, where it would pick up more passengers and cargo. I did not realize at that time how significant that was for me. You see, Christopher Columbus was born in Genoa in 1451. I am sure everyone is aware of this great explorer's accomplishments. What a coincidence that was! I should have realized it then as I was, and still am, somewhat of a history buff. The whole experience onboard was driven by my youth and captivated my imagination. There was no time to think about historical periods or prominent explorers. None of us had ever been on any extensive trip outside of the country, with the exception of my father.

We left Genoa after a six hour stop to reach our next destination, which was Lisbon on the coast of Portugal. We said goodbye to the Mediterranean Sea as we passed through the Strait of Gibraltar. This large canal is about eight miles wide at its narrowest point and connects the Mediterranean Sea to the Atlantic Ocean. This channel is much wider than the Strait of Messina, where I had lived for the past nine years. It also separates Gibraltar and Peninsular Spain in Europe from Morocco in Africa. This was a breathtaking experience with beautiful views and definitely one of the most exotic land and water scenes that I was able to witness during my life; it was even more striking at that tender age.

The ship slowed down a bit passing through this strait, which made the whole experience even more enjoyable. We were all viewing this great spectacle and all of a sudden, to make it even more amazing, a school of twenty or thirty dolphins approached the side of our ship and put up quite the airborne acrobatic sea show. Their swimming speed kept up with the pace of our ship as they were flopping in and out of the water in a graceful and synchronized fashion. The sea was so clean and green, enhancing the acrobatic mammals' display. I can only guess that they were probably accustomed to these large ships sailing through these waters and probably enjoyed playing alongside these large vessels. I wonder if these dolphins' shows are still seen today.

We arrived in Lisbon early in the afternoon. The ship was going to stay anchored there overnight and leave in the early morning. Passengers were allowed to get off the ship if they wished to see the surrounding sights in the vicinity. We took that opportunity to enjoy a stroll on land visiting the nearby shops. My father treated all of us to ice cream as we stopped by a local café. This would be the last time that we would stand on European soil for a long while. I wasn't aware that it would be a long time before I would return to the European mainland.

The ship started the Atlantic crossing early in the morning. We would not see land again for about five days. The ship had plenty of space to walk around when the weather was good, and there was plenty of food available at each daily meal. During our second day at sea, early in the morning as we all were having breakfast in one of the restaurants, a tall young man dressed in a sailor uniform, white pants, shirt, shoes, and sailor hat, approached us at our table. He briefly introduced himself as the Ship's Captain Emissary. He relayed a message to my father, but really to all of us, that the captain would like to host us in the captain's reception room for coffee and dessert that afternoon. I can only guess that my aunt's father in-law must have been friends with the Ship's Captain for him to offer us this personal invitation. My father and mother gladly accepted the invitation. After all, it is not every day that you get an invitation from a captain of an ocean liner bound for America. If I stretch my imagination, that invitation for coffee with the captain was equivalent to us having the opportunity to meet the great Aristotle Onassis. Onassis was the Greek shipping tycoon and our ship was flying the Greek flag.

My mother went to work to prepare us kids for this much-anticipated event. She made sure that we were all dressed well with combed hair. Pretty much all of the things that you would see in the 1960s by a family that wants to deliver a great impression with important and influential people. My siblings and I were told to behave accordingly, to smile, and to just listen to the elders talk. I can still remember her words "I want all of you to be quiet, be respectful, and speak only when asked. Be on your best behavior."

We were escorted to the Captain's Guest quarters by one of his shipmates. He was dressed much like the other shipmate that came during breakfast, but he had a few more stripes on his shirt and arms. Perhaps he was a Quartermaster. As we entered this large room, we were greeted by the Captain and his first mate.

Everyone was introduced to the Captain, and after a brief chat, he walked us closer to the front windows of this grandiose guest room. In actuality, it looked more like a small ballroom. The large room was directly in the center of the ship; it was probably just below the bridge. Parallel to the windows, there was a large impeccably decorated dinner table, probably seating at least twelve people comfortably. On the top of the table were beautiful large china plates filled with cookies, flowers, the now famous Baci chocolates, and other small desserts. Coffee and sodas were also placed on top of the table. All around, there were small serving plates, coffee cups, and cloth napkins next to each place setting. Around the table, there were two large couches and two richly designed soft cloth chairs along the sides. But what caught everyone's attention was the large panoramic view right in front of us, overlooking the bow of the ship and the immense Atlantic Ocean in front of it. The ship was navigating smoothly, breaking through the water as it propelled itself forward. You could see the ship's bow moving through the ocean softly, sinking in and then emerging out of the waves because the sea was not completely serene. It was utterly majestic! There was only water and more water in front of us as far as the eye could see. It was a sunny day, and the shadow of the ship could be seen chasing itself on one side of the ship.

My father and mother carried on a spirited conversation with the Captain, including a discussion of my father's experiences working at the Messina Rodriquez shipyard for the last nine years. The Captain was very kind to me and my siblings. He served us the soft drinks and fancy pastries for us to enjoy while the adults chatted and sipped on their coffee. I believe our visit lasted maybe one hour. My parents thanked the Captain for his kind hospitality as we left that gorgeous room. This was my first wonderfully memorable experience as we journeyed to America. The captain diligently asked one of his officers to accompany us to the main deck and down to our cabin area. Dinner would be served soon on the ship and my mother wanted us to get ready to attend that night's meal before retiring to our quarters.

The five-day Atlantic crossing was uneventful except for one night. It must have been our fourth day when our ship encountered extremely rough seas. As we were walking to the dining room for lunch, the ship erratically moved up and down and swayed from side to side. As we passed through the hallways, the crew had placed large soft red ropes on the sides to help passengers stabilize themselves as they walked along. Everyone was moving in and about by holding their hands on these ropes to support their footing and hopefully mitigate any falls or slipups.

We barely made it to the dining room that day, and not many people showed up due to the rough motions of the ship. My father told us not to eat too much and also to drink small amounts of water. He knew about sea sickness since he had seen it in many scenarios while working and testing the hydrofoils, often on rough seas. He was not shaken by any of this, but for us it was an entirely different ordeal.

When we finally went back to our cabin that night, things got even worse. I looked out of our two small windows and could see that it was raining quite hard. Water was profusely pouring down the outsides of the windows. It was getting dark outside, and we could not see much of anything out there. The sound of the waves impacting the ship's bottom hull would rebound every couple of seconds. It was a thumping sound punishing the body of the ship as she was cruising, breaking through those big waves that mercilessly pushed her to challenge her seaworthiness.

I recall that it was almost midnight, and nobody could sleep. There was just too much motion for us. My little brother and sister were also acting up, sometimes crying and probably experiencing seasickness. For my part, I was not in any better shape. I was experiencing nausea and having a hard time holding down what little I had for dinner a few hours earlier. My father was playing the doctor figure in the cabin, telling us not to move around too much or it would make us feel worse. My mother wasn't in a very good mood, either. She only had coffee and toast for dinner. Obviously, she knew better than us.

The ship was still in the middle of that storm, and there was no relief in sight. I had fought for hours to keep the little food that I had from refluxing out, but I knew I was losing the battle. I called my father, who was on the opposite side of the cabin, and told him that I had to go to the bathroom. He came, lifted me up, and pulled me down to the floor since I was on the top bunk. He brought me directly to that little bathroom in our cabin. Not even a second too soon in that room, I spewed everything right into the toilet bowl. One more second, and it would have been all over the cabin floor.

Finally, when night became morning, the weather subsided, and the waves flattened from their peak. As I looked out the cabin window, I could see brightness peeking through the clouds far off on the horizon. It was mid-morning when the seas finally calmed down substantially, and the sun was breaking through the clouds. I can only say that it was "a night to remember" for the rest of my life, and with God's help, everyone survived this ordeal.

It was now the last day in the Atlantic Ocean, and we were to anchor in Halifax, Nova Scotia, in the early morning. We would finally land on the North American continent: our last stop before we reached our final destination: New York! The ship arrived in the Port of Halifax early next morning, and everyone was allowed to leave the ship for a few hours, but we had to remain in the containment portion of the port infrastructure. It was nice to step on solid ground but the first thing that we noticed was the chilling temperature outside; it was late October. My mother had put aside our light winter coats if you wanted to call them that. You see, winter in Sicily was quite mild compared to the temperatures that we found in the northern part of the North American continent. This was our introduction to the fresh, new, and invigorating climate that would be with every one of us for a large part of our adult lives.

The ship left late that evening, headed for the port of New York. The next day, early in the morning of October 27, 1967, our ship entered our final destination at the mouth of the Hudson River. What awaited us at the entrance of the port of New York was what we all have been seeing for decades at the movies or on television. Yes, it was her: The Statue of Liberty. The most beautiful and majestic woman in the world and the awe-inspiring sign of freedom. As the ship slowly entered the port of New York, she looked even more beautiful than in the books or on-screen. There she was: overpowering the size of our ocean liner, standing tall on that land called the United States of America.

The Statue of Liberty is everything and more than what has been written, described, and said about her. She is a welcoming beacon of reassurance, confidence, prosperity, freedom, and liberty to everyone that passes by her. There are no words that can explain what you feel inside when you are finally face to face with her. Everyone on the ship was silent as we slowly passed by her. The silence was suddenly broken by the ship's mighty horn, breaking the morning haze at the entrance of the port. This could have been in recognition of entering the port of New York as we sailed by that awesome statue. Two large tugboats approached our ship to accompany us slowly to our dock. No matter what, I knew that our ship's horn saluted Lady Liberty and said to her "Good morning, your Highness, here I bring more immigrants to you yet again, yearning to start their new life in America" and "I ask you to bless them, keep them safe, give them health, happiness, and prosperity. They will repay you in time with their hard work as their gift to you, which will make America even greater than today, October 27, 1967."

I would like to stop now, take a deep breath since I am almost in tears, and present in this portion of my writing the feelings that I am experiencing in reliving that moment in my history as a young immigrant. For most of you readers that were born in America, the above paragraph may seem uneventful. But for someone like me and many millions of others that had the opportunity of being welcomed to America by the Statue of Liberty, it is an overwhelming, awesome, incredible experience. Today in the year of our Lord 2023, that day still lives in me, and gives me comfort and hope that the America that I experienced on that day over fifty years ago will always be there and guide me forever. I don't want to scold any of my readers that may not share some of my thoughts. There are some days, currently, when

I have a hard time recognizing the America that greeted me on that sunny day in 1967. Too many people like us have worked too hard and some have died in making our American dream a reality. Let's not lose track of what this America and our great Constitution have imparted on all of us, those inalienable rights that cannot be found in any other country in the world.

We disembarked the ship and headed toward the exit. But there was one more door to go through before we could reach the port exit and become part of the American dream. This was the immigration department window, where the authorities were waiting for everyone to certify and review all of our papers and credentials. The immigration authorities asked my father many questions, among them where he planned to live initially, including the address and the city where we would be heading. The names of relatives, if any, that we will be staying with and their relationship to us. When all was finally squared away, the immigration agent welcomed all of us to America and directed us to the exit of the New York port of entry. I want my reader to remember that when we arrived in America, the American Consulate in Italy had already issued all of us our Green Alien cards that so many foreigners are yearning to get.

We became one of the many millions of *legal immigrants* admitted to the United States of America in this last century. My mother's first cousin Joe, and his father, my great uncle, had driven to New York to pick us up outside the gates of that port of entry. My mother quickly saw them and all of us walked toward that waiting area just outside the exit gates. We all embraced each other, even if my siblings and I did not know who they were. They welcomed us to America in our native Italian language. There was a multitude of other immigrant families being greeted by their loved ones all around us. This reminded me of those films when people finally get off at the train station, and their friends, relatives, or lovers can't wait to see them again, hug, and kiss them. I must confess, I did experience that emotion one other time in my personal life, as I traveled to a foreign place, now one of my *favorite Caribbean islands. It is an awesome feeling.*

I had never met Joe before, but I did somewhat recall his father who visited us in Sicily several years earlier. The whole experience for me seemed like an exotic trip, but instead, it was much more serious. This was going to be our new home country. Our new-found relatives would drive us home to Boston, which was our final destination. To my surprise, Joe came with a glamorous and grandiose American car; at least, that was my impression. This vehicle was one of those big, dazzling American cars that I saw many times on TV and at the movies in Italy. It had a long wing on each side of the rear luggage compartment, and it looked like a jet plane. It was so big that my sister, brother, mother, and I would comfortably fit in the back seat. In the front, my father was also comfortably sitting with Joe, the driver, and his father in the middle. We were able to put all three of our bags in that huge rear trunk. The big boxes that traveled with us on the ship would be delivered to Boston via truck in the next few days. I still remember the incredible soft ride in that car. It was like no other car that I ever experienced. I could tell that it had a strong engine pulling it swiftly on the beautiful highway just outside New York that we crossed on our way to Boston. I was overwhelmed by the huge highway lanes and how everyone was driving, observing their lane travel and not rushing to overtake a slower-driving car. What a contrast to the chaotic way Italians drove their cars in Italy, always passing, beeping, and accelerating to overtake a slower-moving car.

It was a very relaxing trip. We were able to enjoy some of the countrysides during some of the highway sections while my parents were chatting with our American relatives. I later discovered that the car was an early 1960s Cadillac four-door sedan, probably a De Ville. It was a loaner that my cousins borrowed from one of their machine shop clients. It was very nice of

Cousin Joe to make our first American experience so memorable and glamorous. I will never forget it.

Today I own and drive two beautiful German cars after owning many American cars. This is reminiscent of my father's legacy, always talking about those perfectly running German engines, but I am always reminded that it all started with that big, beautiful American-made Cadillac. I don't take anything for granted today. As you continue reading this book, you will see that it was not an easy road for any of us to achieve our identity in America. We will encounter massive mountains to climb, many rivers to cross, and countless roads to travel, some very smooth but some very rocky. It was the beginning of our new life in America. Some of the upcoming narratives of our life in America may disturb some of the readers. It was not as easy, as you may imagine it was. These are all true recollections of our interactions with people, places, and the American dream.

Once we arrived at our Boston destination, we were guests of my mother's cousins until we could secure our own apartment. They all owned and lived in a three-family home in a suburb just a few miles north of Boston. I had never seen a house like that; they do not exist in Italy, and I was very impressed by the construction of the homes that I found in Boston. Almost all of them were built with a wooden structure, unlike the solid brick-and-mortar construction of our apartment building in Messina. What I really liked was that every home, no matter how big or small, had a little plot of land around it, which was part of that house's property. My mother's cousins were the sons and daughters of my grandfather Vincenzo's brother Ciccio. They had also lived in Tripoli but immigrated to America in the early 1950s; I spoke of them in the previous portion of this book.

My grandfather Vincenzo and his brother Ciccio, together in Italy 1960s.

But now I think it is time to understand and come full circle as to how these relatives found themselves in Boston and under what circumstances they immigrated. My mother's cousins found themselves in the United States due to my grandfather Vincenzo's move to Boston in 1919. I detailed earlier in the book about his short stay in America and some of his experiences in Boston. My grandfather decided not to stay in America after spending several years working in Boston. This was simply his personal preference. However, during that time in Boston, even if things did not work out for him, he thought about his other siblings that were living in Tripoli. He prepared the necessary documents and made it possible for his two sisters and a brother to join him in America. You may remember these were the sisters that eventually opened a variety store in the late 1940s in the suburbs of Boston. The store initially grew very fast and they eventually found themselves in a situation that required hiring some outside help. To make matters worse, they were unable to bear any children of their own. So, they reached out to their remaining brother, Ciccio, who was still in Tripoli. They were aware that Ciccio had lost his wife due to a tragic accident and that his young teenage kids were growing up without a mother. Their father was barely keeping up with his parental duties.

One of the two sisters contacted Ciccio and offered to take in his twin sons and provide them with a mother figure, a stable home, and a secure life. They would grow up in a real Italian home in exchange for helping out in the store after school and on weekends. Ciccio could visit them anytime. That left him to concentrate on bringing up his younger daughters, that stayed behind for now. Ciccio agreed to send his young boys to America, recognizing their opportunity for a better future while enjoying a full family life with his sisters.

Those young boys and their sisters, who also eventually made their way to America, are my mother's first cousins. At the time, they had been living in Boston for almost fifteen years. They enjoyed a nice life of their own, thanks to their aunt's kindness. This really emphasizes the full circle of life, the extended family that once existed, helping the next generation to move forward into the future. This reunion for my mother with her first cousins in the United States was the first time they had seen each other since they had all lived in Tripoli during the 1950s.

Even before our arrival, my mother's cousins had already made some housing arrangements for us. They made a tentative arrangement for us, pending our inspection and approval, to rent a nearby apartment. An Italian family had arrived a few years earlier from Italy and they had just purchased a three-family house about one mile from our cousin's home. They met via a mutual friend and became aware that they had the first-floor apartment empty and available to be rented. Our cousins thought that it would be a great match and opportunity for us as newcomers to live there since the owners were also Italian immigrants. The owners also preferred to have an Italian family occupy the apartment if it was possible. My father and mother looked at the apartment a few days after our arrival and agreed to take it and move there as soon as possible. It is very important for any family to identify a place to call their home, especially when so many other things are all up in the air. A home is a place where all the issues and problems of everyday life are neutralized. The family can find comfort and reassurance within its boundaries. These were some of the basic teachings by which my parents brought me up. My father obviously wanted to establish some stability, and a steady home was the starting point.

We stayed with our newly found relatives for about ten days, which was useful for making the move-in preparations and buy some basic furniture for our new apartment. Our cousins were very hospitable with us and since they occupied the three floors of the house, we were able to split up and stay on the different floors with plenty of space. My siblings were accommodated with the cousins' younger kids, who were similar in age. I stayed with my parents in one of the other apartments. What was neat about the whole situation was that everyone was going up and down between each of the homes many times during the day. We were spending time at the different apartments occupied by each family since they were all brothers and sisters. The families were comprised of two twin brothers, each married with two young kids. These were the two brothers that came to America to help their aunt with the food market in the early 1950s. They lived on the first and second floors, while one of their sisters lived on the third floor with her husband.

Everyone was now a naturalized American citizen. They started their own business many years ago, which was a machine shop, and they had already achieved a nice comfortable life. I could not believe that we finally had some close relatives to talk to and share our lives with. It was a substantial difference from our previous life in Sicily, where we only had my mother's sisters and a couple of close friends. This initial experience was wonderful for my parents. They could finally talk about their old times in Tripoli, when they were all much younger while acquainting themselves with their new American life. For my part, I really did not have anyone close to my age among all the kids. My sister and brother found new friends with my mother's cousins' sons and daughters that were much closer to their age. I was almost thirteen, and I considered myself closer to the adults than the younger ones. By listening to these new-found families and their conversations, I had the opportunity to learn so much that I didn't know about my parents' lives, especially during their earlier years before they got married. Those conversations actually helped me substantially to write the two previous sections of this book.

My mother and her cousins grew up together in Tripoli. They shared stories about the war in North Africa and how their parents kept them safe during those dark times. When the war reached the African land, their parents paid to have small ships bring them back to the Italian mainland to their uncle's home in Sicily. The war, as we know, actually proceeded to the Italian mainland, where they found themselves trapped as the war ravaged on. They experienced life-threatening situations during those times in Italy. I recall them telling one story of a very close call of them nearly being killed inside their uncle's house. The American Air Force bombarded their small town during a night raid, and by morning, only a few homes were left untouched. By some miracle, their uncle's house was spared. They said that that was the scariest night of their lives. Most of the homes in that town were destroyed, and many people died. I also remembered my father telling our neighbor when we were living in Messina of his close encounters with death during the war. But to hear it now from our cousins here in America brought a whole new perspective of what my family endured during those dark years of the Second World War.

On a lighter note, I was most intrigued by listening to our cousins recount their early days when they arrived in America. I paid much attention to them because I thought that they could be an introduction to what I may be encountering during my upcoming time here in America. Their shared stories from their past came to be useful to me. It really opened my eyes to this new country and its customs. Unfortunately, and I must say this with a heavy heart, they also mentioned that they saw a lot of vocal immigrant discrimination during the 1960s, something that was non-existent in Italy. This did not apply to the non-white minority only but also to us Italians like me during those days. Nationality discrimination was there for everyone to see, but it was rarely talked about in any open forum. This was kind of swept under the rug by the news in those days; I call it an uncomfortable truth. The news hardly covered it unless someone was killed or some kind of real loss had occurred. It was very likely that in school and other places, you were called offensive names based on your ethnic origin. The Italians were not spared, and nor were the Jews, Irish, Germans, and more. I can testify today, in thinking about those early days in America, that I always believed that America was a great melting pot in the world. America is a great nation that, since its inception, has endured violence and discrimination directed toward different ethnic and racial groups. There are great rewards and opportunities in this melting pot, but they don't come cheap.

I personally encountered many of these situations. Thank God none of them became violent, but they did shake me up a few times. As my life path continues today, many Americans have become very vocal, mostly through technology and social media. In those early days, you had to look into someone's eyes and say it to their face where there was an immediate reaction. It could be positive or negative; you just had to decide how important that was to you. Do I take things into my own hands right now or walk away and wait for another day? Today you can really hurt people electronically from anywhere in the world and incur no repercussions. I was brought up in the honor system. You stand up and look that person in the eye and make your point "Man to Man" or "Man to Woman." It goes back to the Roman days and, as I was told by my parents, if you "Live by the sword, be ready to die by the sword." Today you live by the cell phone and probably will die with that cell phone, hypothetically speaking.

In any case, let's get back to those early days in America. It was good to be with the adults in the room during our family gatherings. I didn't realize how simple and cleaner life was in those days without cell phones, computers, and with very little television. But regrettably, it was never without the walls to climb and rivers to cross; hopefully, you were a good climber and swimmer. As we continue, you will notice many of these metaphors reflected throughout this chapter.

Since it was late October of 1967 when we arrived in America, the school year was almost two months into session. Knowing that I attended a Catholic elementary school in Italy, our cousins convinced my parents that I should be enrolled at the local Catholic elementary school. I have always looked at their decision as the greatest mistake my parents made on my behalf, which forever affected my future.

Let me explain one important thing about American schools in those days. The support for immigrants that did not speak English in the public schools was in its infancy. However, when you paid to enroll in a Catholic elementary school, which should have been better, the language support for non-native English speakers was non-existent. The Catholic schools in America were more interested in religious education than in educating newcomers like me, with no practical skills in the English language being taught. I consider myself to have been caught in one of the biggest failures of the Catholic school system of those days. In retrospect, I can ascertain that all of the schools, parochial, private, and public, were well behind the academic standards of the European school system. The schools are somewhat better today but they still lag behind the European model. The forefront of the American elementary system, grades 1 to 8, is in sharp contrast to the European model. Europe, in general, considers grades 1 through 5 as their elementary school. You may recall that I was attending 7th grade, and I was promoted to attend 8th grade in Messina just before we left for America. I really never went to school that fall because we were leaving Italy about a month into the school year. To my astonishment, everything changed for me when I was put into the American school system. They were not ready for a student like me. As a note, to be fair to today's parochial schools, both my son and my daughter attended private Catholic school in Boston from kindergarten through 12th grade. These schools have made substantial improvements since those early days. Notwithstanding this progress, they still have not caught up in justifying their tuitions, as far as I am concerned.

When my parents met with the school principal at the Catholic school, the mother superior running the school gave my parents a dose of her reality. She communicated to them through my mother's cousins, the translators, that since I was not able to communicate verbally or in any written form in the English language, she would not be inclined to register me in the 8th grade. She defended her decision by declaring that since 8th grade was the last year of elementary school, and due to my English language issue, I would not be ready to attend the next grade, which was considered the first year of high school in America. She also pointed out that it was almost November, and school started two months ago. She argued that I missed some critical learning exposure in those first two months. What critical learning was she talking about? I knew that I couldn't put a sentence together or speak more than a few words. That had absolutely nothing to do with the "critical learning phase." What a load of crap that was, but those were the late 1960s, and the immigrants had to plow their own road.

My parents were convinced that it was better for me to return and repeat the 7th grade again. How can I, today, be rational and calm in recalling my survival and the sacrifices of a young man exposed at the age of thirteen to this new and foreign country? Please standby, it gets even more fascinating as I share the experiences of that incredible first school year in America and beyond.

At the same time, our family needed to start building our new life in America and that started with my father's new job. You may recall that our cousins were able to contact one of their clients, a local trucking company in need of an experienced diesel mechanic. This company decided to sponsor my father with a work contract under the current immigration guidelines since they were unable to find a qualified person to serve the needs of their business. This work contract helped us to somewhat speed up our immigration request even if our acceptance still dragged on for well over a year. I can say plainly today that the past immigration system not only favored close-blood relatives to reunite and immigrate to America, but it also leveraged a merit system to complement this process. It prioritized individuals that were seen as essential to American companies in keeping them competitive and successful.

We had finally moved and settled into our new first-floor apartment. My father reported for work on the Monday morning of the following week. A striking discovery was made when he reported for work with the owner of the trucking company. To my father's astonishment, his job required him to work what you may call the graveyard shift: 7:00 PM – 3:00 AM. I can only imagine what a letdown that must have been for my father to discover the hourly details of his new job in America. He had never worked those hours on any regular basis other than when he and his fellow mechanics had to complete emergency repairs on disabled ships in Messina. That happened only two or three times during all his time at the shipyard, and he was compensated very handsomely for those overtime hours. This was the beginning of our discovery of America and the first lesson for my father to learn, which must have been bittersweet; he learned that American businesses never sleep. His job maintaining the trucks could not be done during the regular work day; it had to be done at night when they were parked in the garage. This allowed the trucks to be serviced and made operational, ready to be used the next morning.

Let's analyze the situation that was presented to my father and our family. It was now mid to late November in Boston. The weather was not what we were used to in Italy, and to make things even more difficult, his work schedule ended in the wee times of the morning. My father had no car. In fact, he did not even have a driver's license, and he had to rely on public transportation even if this job was only five or six miles away from our home. The busses often didn't run after 8:00 PM, and the wait for transportation in those cold temperatures must have been quite a hardship. What a far cry this job was from what he had left behind, but my father endured. As we say, he sucked it up, for better or for worse.

I recall that during those early days, things were not too calm in our new home. My parents argued often and it was all about our new life in America and the circumstances that we were faced with. The language barrier, the transportation issues, the cold weather, the environment, and the people: everything was very unfriendly and intimidating to all of us. This reminded me, and probably my mother, of a déjà vu from when we moved from Tripoli to Messina but by a factor of 10. Thanks to God, we were able to befriend the landlord who spoke Italian, and together with our nearby cousins, we were able to endure some of these hurdles as best we could. If we didn't have this extended family support, I think things would have been quite disastrous for everyone.

I really wonder how a family these days can land in America all alone and deal with their new life and needs. Most of the time, these new immigrants have no job initially and very little skills. They have no extended family and many of them also don't speak any English. If it was difficult for us with many of these necessities already in place, I shudder at what these new immigrants have in store. I can only conclude that their previous life was so bad that any alternative would be an improvement, no matter the cost.

But since I am on this subject, has anybody asked themselves or to our leaders about our costs? The cost to America? I am a firm believer that an immigration merit system like the one that my family benefitted from is the correct means to a successful immigration system. I know that the United States is a large country and full of opportunities, but we cannot contain all of the people of the world in our country. If all of the countries would unite under a somewhat free and democratic system similar to ours, then we would not need borders. We would just have one country all around us. But unfortunately, our standards, the justice, economic, cultural, and government systems are not accepted by many of these countries, especially the ones that many immigrants come from. Thus, in order to retain our nation and ideals, we must be respectful but also very specific in whom we allow to come here to live. All we need to remember and say very often is, *"I pledge allegiance to the Flag of the United States of America, and to the Republic for which it stands, one Nation under God, indivisible, with liberty and justice for all."*

Late November brought some calmness and eased some of our tension all due to an American holiday that we had never experienced before: Thanksgiving! I learned that Thanksgiving is always observed on the last Thursday of November. This was almost a month after our arrival in America. Since it occurs on Thursday, many people would also take Friday off from work, if possible, and make it a really nice long, festive weekend. It is a solemn yet cheerful day when families gather together to give thanks and celebrate with a wonderful feast. The large bird, a turkey, is featured as the main course as a sign of prosperity. I learned that the symbol behind this beautiful and quite elaborate meal was initially started by the early settlers of America. After they were able to harvest a good crop during the autumn, the early settlers of the original American colonies gathered together to give thanks for this new land. They would use a turkey to celebrate their arrival and good harvest since wild turkeys were very plentiful in New England. We were able that year, and for many more after that, to unite with my mother's cousins at their three-family home or at ours to celebrate this wonderful new holiday. It really took some of the edge off of our life, which during that initial period was putting our family in an unpleasant situation due to the pressures that I penned earlier.

My father had a one-year work contract, and he was paid quite well, above the average pay grade at the time. I believe he endured his work without a car until Christmas, but following the holidays he had to buy one. It was necessary for him so that he could commute back and forth to work in the middle of the frigid New England winter. In the late 1960s, there was no written test given by the Registry of Motor Vehicles in any language except English. This meant that it was very hard for my father to pass the written exam. Remember that this was the age before computers; there was only paperwork. It is my understanding that our cousins knew someone at the Registry of Motor Vehicles. This individual was able to get a certificate that he passed the written test and after he took a road test, he acquired a driver's license. I am sure this was some kind of compensatory transaction, but this is what it took then to get a license, especially if you had the means but no practical knowledge of the English language. Everyone today takes it for granted that these tests are now available in multiple foreign languages. The hardship is pretty much gone, but in those times, it was quite a bridge to cross.

My father was finally able to purchase a car by coupling his savings with a local bank loan. I think it was always my father's dream to buy a Ford. He recalled that his American co-workers at the American base in Tripoli always said that a Ford was the best car built in the United States. Not only did he purchase a Ford, he bought what was considered the ultimate American family car: a station wagon. I can still picture that massive car that thwarted our Fiat 500 in Italy. This thing was so big that you could actually lay down and sleep comfortably behind the back seat.

The acquisition of the car took some weight off my father's shoulders for dragging the whole family to America. Yet, my mother would always remind him during many other family squabbles that, no matter what, he should have listened to me and come alone to America to see it firsthand. She told him that he would have lasted maybe thirty days once he fully realized what he was up against: the job and everything else. She told him that he would board the next plane back to Italy to ask for his old job back. As you can see, this matter was a very contentious subject during our family conversations. I always felt throughout my adulthood that my mother made a point of reminding my father that he had made a big mistake by "Coming to America." This may sound peculiar, but it explains why I elected to name this part of my book exactly that. It reflected our journeys and experiences of the last fifty years. My father, being a man of his word, was always faced with the challenge of providing a better life for everyone and that was his primary goal for the rest of his life. He trusted and believed in the American spirit and that dream would eventually overcome all of the obstacles presented to us.

Unfortunately, during those initial months, and probably years, this was a distant dream. My father worked hard during those early years to prove that, notwithstanding the sacrifices and bridges to cross, we would eventually cross the finish line. One weekend while we were all gathered at the dinner table, probably six months after we arrived, he told my mother that he spoke to the owner of the trucking company. He told him that he was very grateful for his sponsorship, which made his immigration process move rapidly and allowed him to come to America with a job at hand. But he also told him that he had never worked that late night shift in his life and was not aware of any mention of that in his work contract with him. At the end of his meeting, he told him that he could no longer work those hours and would have to find another job if he couldn't be moved to the daytime shift. The owner, unfortunately, couldn't accommodate him, despite sympathizing with him as a father with young children.

A few weeks later, my father did leave his first job. He was offered the same line of work with a much larger and growing trucking company, and, yes, he was back working the day shift like most people. The newly purchased car allowed him to commute a little further out for this new job. I believe that he also was given a better hourly wage and benefits. It is my understanding that this trucking company was eventually purchased to be part of a larger national company, which became to be known today as United Parcel Service (UPS). But, by that time, my father had already moved on to yet another even better job, let's just say to other newly discovered horizons just to keep everyone hanging.

We are halfway through 1968, the school year is just about finished for me, and pretty much nothing was really accomplished during that time. I spent most of my time in the back of each classroom, moving between two different rooms every day. I wasn't properly comprehending the English language, and I wasn't given any personal, after-school help. The school principal told my parents that she could not promote me to the 8th grade. She used the same excuse as before: this is the final year before high school.

The principal said that she was advised by my two teachers, the first, a nun, and the other, an outside employed educator, that I was not able to understand much of that year's scholastic work. Thus, she could not recommend me to move on to the 8th grade. I hardly completed my homework most of the time, with the exception of mathematics. Here, I excelled since the math taught in 7th grade was very primitive in comparison to what I was taught in Italy.

This hit me like someone had just stabbed me in the back, and I felt helpless to defend myself. My parents must have felt the same way; their dream of a better life in America for us must have been also shattered by this decision. I believe that they should have just taken me out of that horrific school and put me in the public school where I am sure they would have placed me in the eighth grade. We did not talk much that particular day, but it did take a heavy toll on me throughout all my life. That decision to send me to a private Catholic school, which everyone thought would be best for me, had backfired. The school was not equipped for foreign student attendance. In fact, I was the only one there at that time. Paying for a failure to educate anyone, no matter their circumstances, is something that should have weighed a lot in the Catholic education system of those days. Unfortunately, checks and balances were not in place to screen those private institutions in those days. There were very nimble accreditation committees to speak of. I found out much later, when I finally attended public high school, that there were more resources available to foreign students in the public sector, but we failed to take advantage of it because we were immigrants that did not know any better. My parents were led to believe that Catholic education was much better for me. Regrettably, they were new to America and already overwhelmed by surroundings, language, work, and home responsibilities, so they failed to investigate my educational needs. They relied on other people who were also new immigrants themselves without an extensive educational background, and the results were demoralizing. My sister fared much better than me. She attended a small all-girls Catholic school in the same town. She was in the 3rd grade during that same year, but, unlike me, she was promoted to the 4th grade. Obviously, those initial elementary school years didn't carry a lot of weight.

The summer of 1968 was not a great summer for me. I felt unaccomplished and stripped of my intelligence by a school that did not rise to the occasion. I thought about the next scholastic year. The students that I spent almost seven months with would now be in 8th grade, and I would be repeating 7th grade. My bitterness was real, but I could not talk about it with my parents. They were trying their best to adjust to our new life. I felt powerless. In retrospect, I should have asked somebody to get me out of that school and enroll me in the public school. But nobody was competent or aware of the educational system in America; it was just overwhelming. We were now living in America, and we had to play by their rules, while our family members all had the same obstacle: the English language.

My father, on the other hand, was really excelling with his new work. The English language that he was exposed to during his life in Tripoli came back to him much quicker and helped him get ahead. The new job was more of what he was used to, and the hours were 7:00 AM to 4:00 PM, Monday through Friday. He would occasionally work some overtime, but not more than once a week. Nonetheless, he was always home for dinner at 6:30 PM.

What I really liked about the American way of life was the concept of the weekend. We were not used to that in Italy because most people worked at least half a day on Saturday. The day when everyone was home was on Sunday, which is not much of a weekend. I loved the idea of everyone being home doing things on Saturday, such as going out to the stores or the food market, which I was not very fond of. See, our culture pretty much assumes that the woman of the house knows what is necessary for food. She knows who likes what and what needs to be replenished. But the idea that you would go out every day to buy food, like in Italy, went out the window. Just by looking at the size of the American family refrigerator tells you that it was designed to hold more than one- or two days worth of food. So, our family, like everyone else, bought the bulk of our food for the week on Saturdays. There were not many supermarkets around our city, plus my mother was not a big fan of them at the time. Therefore, my father would drive my mother to the Italian section of Boston, known as the North End, every Saturday. She would buy the meat at the Italian butcher shop, the fish at the fish market if she found it to be fresh, cheese and cold cuts at the Italian deli, and the vegetables at the farm stand. If she had plans to invite her cousins over or if we were to visit them, she would also buy some Italian pastries. Every other week she would shop at the large food store to buy canned goods, cereal, eggs, beverages, and all the rest of the nonperishable items. Since we had a local family-owned food store nearby, she would use it to buy small items that were needed or missed during her Saturday excursions.

I want to reiterate that my father was earning good money then, more than the average blue-collar worker of the late 1960s. Good quality food was essential for us, like most Italians, and money was not a factor. Food in my house was always abundant and available and, fortunately, our clan never had a weight issue. Considering that my mother always cooked a two-course meal with sides when home every day, we should have had some weight issues, but our Mediterranean diet, and possibly our genes, likely prevented this.

I can still remember when that station wagon pulled in front of that triple-decker. My father would come into the house with a couple of food bags in his hands. He would find me wherever I was and say, "Go outside and help your mother bring all the bags in." I would find the back of that station wagon full of at least ten additional large paper bags since no plastic bags were around then. I had to make a least three trips, carefully going up the few stairs on the front porch and placing all of them neatly on the kitchen floor. Boy, was I glad that we lived on the first floor of that triple-decker! Imagine if we lived on the second or third floor! I would have probably been an athlete and not in my current occupation.

I must say that I should have enjoyed more of those days and the events; it was a great time because the family was really there. My siblings were very young and would have been playing in their room or on the back porch. I would help my mother put things away in the pantry and also clean up the refrigerator of any leftovers that she thought went bad. I did not like to discard that food. You must realize by now that there were very few electric garbage disposals in the 1960s. Some of you may also remember that many homes in that part of New England had a metal basket inserted inside a ground container, usually in a corner of the backyard. We had one of these behind our back porch that you would open by pushing a foot pedal. You would discard spoiled food in the basket. Many times, I had the chore to go outside and dispose of our garbage there. Thankfully, my mother always put that food in a small bag first to minimize the odor, and during the summer months, she would keep it in the refrigerator until the day before pickup. The sanitation department would come by with their garbage truck twice a week, come inside the yard, take the basket, and dump the contents in their truck. Wow, what a smelly truck that was! You could smell it way before it came to your home. The sanitation workers really endured and were a special kind of people to do that kind of work.

I spent that summer mostly going to the library and trying to learn as much English as I could. I realized then that if I didn't help myself, nobody would. I had to make the best of my current situation, which was a bitter pill to swallow. My mother's cousins did a lot to make us feel at home in this new uncharted, and enchanted land. They organized small weekend trips to the nearby beaches of northern Massachusetts and to the mountains of

New Hampshire. I still remember the first time that we went to the beach in a city about thirty-five miles north of Boston called Gloucester. It was known as a commercial fishing town and many Italian immigrants made their living there by fishing the rich seas off the coast of this New England town. There were many old fishing boats in the harbor with nets and lobster traps. These boats showed many signs of the punishment endured by the harsh ocean waves and wind that engraved their hulls. It was now summer; I could only imagine what it was like enduring the long, cold New England winter, which I just had the pleasure to witness in our first year.

Further down the road from the harbor, there are several beautiful sandy white beaches. I recall one of these beaches named Long Beach. I could see where the name was derived from since it was quite long, maybe a mile, with white sand softly curving around the shore. The end of it softly wrapped into a long arch that ended in a small inhabited little island. During high tide, this land became an island because a canal would fill with sea water, dividing it from the beach. I was astonished by these large differences in sea-water levels between high and low tides. The Mediterranean Sea tide levels were not that drastic in Sicily, but this was the Atlantic Ocean, and there was no comparison.

The Atlantic Ocean in New England had one more hidden surprise for me. The first time that we ventured to this beach with our cousins, it was one of the first truly hot beach days: a beautiful Sunday in mid-June. The weather was sunny and maybe eighty-five degrees. The sand was quite hot yet tolerable to bare feet. I could not wait to jump into that green ocean water since this would be my first time. It was customary in Messina that we would run from the sand and jump straight into the water without stopping, experiencing a refreshing cool down and a speedy swim. I noticed that a lot of people were in the water, but they were just standing there up to their hips, and very few were swimming. To me, it was unusual to see that scene. In Italy, many people would be swimming, and many of them would be in all the way up to their chest or shoulders. I didn't think much of it and I asked my younger cousins that were with me if they wanted to jump into the water. They said, "No, you go for now; we will come in after."

I started to run toward the ocean, probably to show them that I did not fear the water. As I ran into the first couple of feet of the ocean water, I was shocked by how cold it was! This was not the nice, refreshing warm water of the Mediterranean! It was the icy cold water of the northern Atlantic Ocean! I could not retreat from my run now. Every cell in my body was shocked, saying to me, "Get out now!" But I could not. I would not look very macho. I let my whole body fall into the water. My face and head felt like they became an ice cube. I stood up and decided to casually walk out toward the beach, giving up on swimming. I had just learned that the Atlantic Ocean, at least in that part of America, was not going to be my friend for many years to come.

When I walked back out and reached my younger cousins, they were surprised that I did that. "Wow," they said, "you are very brave! The water is cold this time of the year." I asked them why the water was so cold. "Well," they said, "it gets a little bit warmer in late July and August, maybe seventy degrees depending on the currents." "Are you kidding?" I responded. That was still cold, but right now, it felt as though it was in the 60s. I was freezing, and my body was shaking. If not for that sunny, hot day, I would have caught pneumonia.

I ran back to where the adults had made their base camp to get a towel from my mother to dry myself. My mother walked towards me when she saw me approaching their chairs and the beach umbrellas. She got up and said in Italian, "Ma sei pazzo! Are you crazy? The water is freezing here! Don't you know this is the cold Atlantic Ocean? What you think this is, the warm water of Messina?" I spent the rest of the day just playing on the beach and barely touching the water.

As I recollect and write about that now distant first year in America, I am sitting here today in my current home in Southeast Florida right on the Intercostal. The time is about the same - mid-June - and the weather here is much like that of Sicily: sunny, hot, and steamy, just like those summer afternoons on that small balcony in Messina. I must say that I do enjoy going to the beach to swim in the Atlantic Ocean, which is twenty degrees warmer in Florida than that in New England. I am also reminiscing about my life now. I was able to accomplish a nice, quiet way of life and live in a place in America where the ocean water is just as warm as that sea in Sicily. My surroundings may not resemble those of Sicily, but I can definitely say today, as an American citizen, one thing. I endured many sorrows, twisted turns, and giant bridges to cross, but I finally got as close as I could be to that finish line. I am living the last part of my life in the greatest country in the world with a great economy and in one of the best states in the country: Florida. Maybe I could have been better off in Italy. I will never know, but my father decided my future, and I am forever indebted to him for my past fifty years of wonderful experiences. "Until we meet again, Dad."

The following year, I was back at that Catholic elementary school, repeating seventh grade. What a shame! Talk about missed opportunities and wasted time, which could have been used to further enrich my life during those years. Fortunately for me, I was able to somewhat grasp a comprehension of the English language by then. I was understanding most of the readings in the classroom, even if I still struggled with writing skills. Math class was very boring for me; the math was just way too rudimentary. Many students were silently struggling with those simple math problems or fractions, not to mention the metric system. I struggled with word problems since I had to translate what they were saying first, then turn them into a mathematical formula so that they could be solved. I could now communicate using full sentences with the other students and carry on a partially comprehensible conversation.

Lunchtime at that Catholic school really had an impact on me. I remember that in the previous year, all I really could do was just sit there and eat the lunch prepared by my mother. I could not really communicate with the other students that first year, but this second year was much different. I was learning the English language and could connect and somewhat express my thoughts with them. As I said, most of the time, my mother gave me a homemade lunch to take to school, but many of the other students bought the school lunch served in the cafeteria, and everyone would buy the milk in the little cardboard cartons. Wow! Milk with lunch? How disgusting that was for me. I only had milk in the morning with coffee and nice Italian cookies for breakfast. I could not drink white milk with lunch food for the life of me. Plus, let's talk about that American bread called "Wonder Bread." Some kids had it with peanut butter and jelly, while others had some kind of fluffy sweet white cream and marmalade. I later learned that this was Marshmallow Fluff, a delicious sandwich delicacy that was invented in Somerville, Massachusetts, and manufactured in Lynn, Massachusetts. But the bread that everyone was eating was no bread to me. It was mushy, soft, and squeezable with no real crust. My bread was hefty with a beautiful crust, purchased at the Italian bakery in Boston. It was paired with nice mortadella or prosciutto plus provolone cheese. That was what I called lunch. The other kids looked at me and used to say to me, "You can bite into that bread without breaking your teeth?" "Oh yes," I said as I worked my way toward the end of the sandwich, which was the best part: the end of the loaf, which was even harder to bite and chew. I am laughing at myself as I write this because now, the Americans have finally discovered and love that crusty Italian bread and also real Italian cold cuts that are now sold in many local food stores. They may not be the real imported ones unless you go to a specialty food store, but many of them come very close to the original. It came as no surprise to me that our real Italian cuisine eventually would catch up with America and vice versa.

I can still remember gym class. When the weather was too cold or rainy to be outside, we would stay inside the school gymnasium. This structure had a large indoor basketball court and that was the place to go, especially on cold winter days. I recall that shiny wooden floor with four basketball hoops. There was a full-sized regulation court and a short lateral one just to practice. I never had the opportunity to play any basketball in Italy. We always played soccer since much of the time, the weather permitted us to play outdoors.

As the school year ended and the summer of 1969 was approaching, I was finally promoted to attend the 8th grade: that final step towards high school. Was I happy now? Not at all. I had just repeated 7th grade three times in my life: once in Italy and twice in America. Did I learn much? Not really, as far as academics go. But I was still way ahead of my peers. All I had to do now was fully master the English language. I had done it all on my own; no tutor, no after-school teachers, no help from my family. Just me. As I look back to those days, I realize now that I persisted and plowed through many adversities and failures, which would help me endure the ones yet to be encountered.

What about my family? How were things going in our household during this time? My father was doing quite well with his new job. We were living comfortably, and my parents were able to put some money aside. Six months later during that year, my mother wanted so much to help the family that she decided to look for a part-time job in a textile factory within walking distance from our home. My mother had never worked in her life. She was a dedicated wife and cared for all of us when we were living in Italy. Her cousins in America did not work; their husbands had their own businesses, and they were somewhat already on their way to living the American dream. They told my mother that many Italian immigrants were working at this textile factory and if she wanted to help her family, many of them were working there part-time. In agreement and with the support of my father, she was able to secure an 8:00 AM to 2:00 PM job in this factory. All of my younger siblings were now in school. My younger brother was in a local private kindergarten school, and my sister was in 4th grade at the Girl's Catholic School. My mother would drop my younger brother at the kindergarten by 8:00 AM, and my sister would go to school with my mother's cousin's two daughters since they attended the same school and grade. Being much older, I would walk to school and by the time all of us got out of school and made it home, either my mother was already there or just walking in from picking up my younger brother at the pre-school. My father was home by 4:30 PM each evening, sometimes earlier, if traffic was light since he started at 7:30 AM each morning.

During that spring of 1970, we were blessed with a new gift offered to us by this great country. We had been renting now for over two years, but thanks to one of my mother's uncles, that lived in Boston for decades, a new dream was about to happen. I was told that Uncle Jack told my father that he would gladly loan him just over one thousand dollars to use as a down payment if he wanted to buy a family home. Since my father had a secure and well-paying job, he would have no problem getting a mortgage from the bank. Uncle Jack said, "If you find something that you like, just let me know, and I will loan you that initial money." Well, you may wonder now who Uncle Jack was. Thanks to my grandfather, Vincenzo, Uncle Jack was one of the two brothers that started their lives in Boston when they were young, sometime in the late 1920s. Our extended family circles back to meet and help my family after almost forty years. Sometimes you wonder if this big mystery of living is all pre-written by God or if it is left up to us in our quest for a better life to make that choice.

As our life went then, one day early in the spring of 1970, a single-family home went up for sale a couple of blocks down the street from my mother's cousins. The asking price was $12,000.00 dollars, but it also needed a lot of work. The house was an old New England-style colonial wooden framed home with three small bedrooms on the second floor. On the first floor, there was a kitchen, living room, dining room and bathroom. A small backyard with a detached one-car garage was also included. The driveway leading to this garage could accommodate two or three cars parked one behind the other. It was on a very quiet dead-end street which exited to the main street of the city. Everything was within walking distance: our schools, my mother's job, and our cousins. This was almost a dream come true, but the house had not been lived in for over a year. The owners had died, and their family took their time to sell it; probably, some legal paperwork was holding up the sale. This home needed a lot of work and materials to make it a nice livable family home. My mother's cousins did not like it too much because it was so rundown, but my father did not flicker a bit. He made an offer of $11,000.00, and we eventually purchased it for $11,100.00. The bank loaned my father ten thousand dollars, and he used Uncle Jack's money for the down payment. As you can guess now, our real American dream had just begun.

This American dream was somewhat short-lived because when we finally took possession of this new home, a dose of reality sank in. This home required a lot more work and materials than my father estimated in order to bring it up to living standards. It would not be a short and easy road to follow, but my father was again unfazed. He decided that we should stay in our rental home for a couple more months until he could clean it up and fix it so that we could live there. This home, unlike the home that we moved into when we arrived in Messina, was not new by any stretch of the imagination. It was built in the 1920s and had been neglected by the previous owners. But to give it some credit, the home was double the size of the apartment we had in Messina. With its three bedrooms, I had to share my room with my younger brother. My sister had her own private bedroom which was also connected to ours by a door. The main entrance to her bedroom was right up from the staircase. My parents had their own private bedroom across from ours all within a small semi-circle of a hallway connecting all these rooms' entrances. The stairway was magnificent by our standards. It needed work, but we had never had one.

The first floor had a good-sized kitchen with a side pantry and a bathroom. I am not sure why these old homes had the only bathroom built right next to the kitchen, but I guess that was standard from that old American construction era. My mother did not like this one bit. She used to say that it was not correct to have a bathroom right off the kitchen, and she was definitely right. But we could not change this layout; the house was built like that, and there was no way to change it. We also had a nice hallway at the front door entrance that led to a beautiful dining room and a living room flowing around it. There was also a gorgeous, curved bay window looking outside to the dead-end street. At the end of this short road and behind a large fence, an uncultivated piece of land and wild grass was visible. An old city commercial railroad existed past that wild patch of land. It probably was used to bring goods to that town maybe fifty years earlier when the town was in its infancy. Actually, the address of our home was not a Street but a Place, very appropriately. This road was called Thorney Place, and our house number was #11. On this very narrow road, maybe 250 feet long, five or six additional homes were located on either side. We also had a nice covered wooden front porch attached to the house extending probably fifteen feet, and a much smaller back door exit with an uncovered porch. Both of these entrances provided very nice access to this little New England colonial home. The driveway was located all along the side of the house, but it also was old and full of overgrown vegetation on the sides and middle. It had two long cement pavers on its left and right for the car to drive on it, with dirt in the middle. The one-car garage also needed a lot of TLC and rehabilitation, but it served as an operational center and storage during my father's rehabilitation of this home. A small backyard was located behind the house next to the side of the garage. Large tall trees were planted around the perimeter with overgrown grass and weeds in the middle.

By the way, did I mention that this house had a basement? Yes, something that we were not accustomed to before. The home's stone foundation was probably five feet below ground level, and this basement was quite large, holding the perimeter of the house. The heating and hot water systems were located within the cellar. A wooden staircase accessible from a kitchen door would bring you up and down from this space. The basement walls were made of raw stone with old cement binding that had seen better days. The basement had a dirt floor with a couple of cement patches, especially under the heating and hot water appliances. This portion of the house reminded me of those scary Hitchcock movies. The interior space was not well-lit at all. I believe it only had two or three electric lamps with a pull string on them. During the day, three or four small rectangular wood-framed windows located on top of the basement wall brought some additional light, especially if it was a sunny day outside. The basement was not meant to be a living space, at least not in the near future. The house was surrounded on the outside by a five-foot chain-link fence all around to divide our land from that of the adjacent neighbors' homes. Not considering the amount of work needed, this was our small, private palace. A beautiful tall cypress tree was located to the left at our entrance. It was a magnificent addition by Mother Nature. It gave the house character and was our home's landmark.

You could say that we always had a large Christmas tree at the entrance of our home all year long.

My father started by replacing all of the wallpaper in the house as per my mother's exquisite and somewhat expensive taste. He painted or stained all of the wooden structures, including the stairs leading to the second floor. When all of the walls and the painting were done, he called a company to sand and stain all the rooms that I thought had very old non-salvageable hardwood floors. But I can still remember the beauty that came out from those wooden floors neglected for at least thirty years. The wood grain and the shine emulating from those floors once the work was done was heart-stopping. They looked like they were just installed. The natural oak color brought much warmth and comfort to the home. Finally, he shined the ceramic floor in the kitchen and bathroom. Everything looked and smelled so good, but it was two or three months of hard work for everyone, especially me, since I was almost sixteen and I became my father's little helper. We all contributed by working late weekday nights when possible and every single weekend doing our part in cleaning up the place after the renovation. I recall the city garbage pickup workers were not happy when week after week, they would find all kinds of material by the side of the road next to our home that my father would store temporarily in the garage. But my father would give them a couple of dollars, and they were happy, as if it was Christmas. You might remember that the average pay in those days was less than $ 2.00 per hour. I believe that my father, at that time, was making almost double that as a diesel mechanic at his new job. He would not work overtime because he had to get home and work on our new home. Those were wonderful times. I did not appreciate working a lot with my father, but I was the only one that could actually help him.

Let me just tell you that my father continued to work on that house for over ten years. When he finally sold it to move to a bigger, newer home, the people that bought it thought it was a fairly new home; everything was updated and renewed. I will move on from our first home story now, but it will intersect many times in this book as time moves on.

I finally graduated from that dreaded Catholic school, and I was now enrolled in 9th grade. My parents finally gave up on the private school concept on my behalf, but they kept my sister at the Catholic school. Since she was much younger, she did not experience the educational losses that I did. It was also time for my younger brother to start school, and he also attended that same school. I was now free from those suffocating institutions. I had finally moved to the city's public school system. That school was also a far cry from the education received in my earlier days in Italy when I attended 6th and 7th grade. But I must say it was definitely a better place to be and learn than the past 2.5 years at the Catholic school. But there is always a catch. When they say, "Don't count your chickens until they hatch," you must believe it. It turned out that the high school in our town was not big enough to accommodate grades 9 through 12. Many years ago, the city divided the 9th grade, the so-called freshman high school grade, into three schools located throughout the city. These schools were extended elementary schools teaching grades 6 to 9. This last grade was called junior high school. Depending on your home's proximity to each of these schools, you were assigned to attend the one that was closest to your home. Fortunately for me, I would be there for only one year and then move to the city's main high school campus. Having now gained a somewhat better understanding of the English language, I can say that I was able to breeze and excel through the 9th grade. During that year, I was spending half of my time at the local library to better myself in subjects that were foreign to me, like English and American history. I was also searching out what I wanted to be and studying for my future. This subject has been a revolving door for me always until I finally was able to be my own boss and own my own company. For now, this was way down the line decades from now. Many laborious circumstances will be in front of me to overcome first, and a lot of hard work, education, and experience to eventually achieve my final destiny.

My father was achieving new goals with his new job, and with the help of my mother's part-time work, the family was putting money in the bank. We were definitely in a much better place than when we first arrived. That extra income contributed to being able to live our new American life in a comfortable fashion. My father always returned home after his eight hours of work; overtime was not his cup of tea. There were other reasons for that, and one was that a couple of times a week and also during the weekend, he would repair friends' and neighbors' cars in our driveway. Just like in Italy, he was earning extra money with these part-time auto repairs. The extra money was mostly used to buy materials to update our home. My father knew how to do much of the work needed on his own, and he was quite good at it. But don't think that he worked all the time. On Sunday, just like in Italy, all of us would get inside that big Ford station wagon and go for long afternoon trips. We would go either north to the countryside in New Hampshire, Maine, or to a beach in the summer, weather permitting. Many times during the year, we would also organize daylong trips to landmark places such as North Conway in New Hampshire or Old Orchard Beach in Maine together with my mother's cousins and their kids. This was an exciting time for me, even if I were a teenager. My younger siblings had the opportunity to be with my mother's cousin's boys and girls who were closer to their age. Our family's nucleolus was very much in place, just like it always was in Italy. The surroundings were much different: the land, trees, and the ocean seemed endless in America. It was not much on the forefront of our minds then, but we were living in the greatest country in the world. We were slowly getting the feel, but we were working diligently every day to earn our piece of the American dream. Everyone was on the same page; it was a team effort, and we were blessed to have at our disposal the means, for that financial stability had always evaded my father until now. It had been a long time coming, but we were now definitely heading in the right direction.

The extended family that we found in Boston played a large part in making our American experience a joyful one. Their close proximity to our home allowed us to spend many weekends together. We would either gather at their home, or they would come to ours. These were extremely fun times, and when we all congregated, there would be a lot of us. There were at least eleven adults and eight children. I considered myself an adult, so did I make that odd number? Everyone's home had very nice little backyards, and we would set up a long table to accommodate all of the adults and a smaller one for the young kids. If the weather or the season did not permit the outside scene, then we would use their three-family home's large, finished basement. Unfortunately, when they came to our home since our basement was unfinished, we used the whole first floor of our house. You can imagine all these Italians talking and eating up a storm! Everyone prepared different dishes or collaborated on a large prearranged menu. One family made the pasta which was always the most elevated food and a grandiose feat, especially among the men. They would say, "You see, you got to have that pasta dish, or else it would not be an Italian meal." The women of each household also made their own contributions. On the table, you would also see the fish dish, some kind of meat or chicken, and sometimes all of them. Let's not forget the many side dishes, salads, and vegetables. All of them had a way of satisfying each person's preference for condiments and recipes.

Let's talk about the wine. You cannot eat an Italian meal without wine; it would not be complete. My mother's cousins, as I said, had the luxury of that large, finished basement below their three-family home. Well, guess what? What else do you think happened in a smaller room next to that? Yes, homemade wine was made, and plenty of it, always red wine. During the fall season in a nearby city where the food wholesalers' market was located, trains and trucks would arrive carrying wine grapes from California. Then, and still today, homemade wine makers would drive there during the wine season to get the grapes at this market. They would go there with their pick-up trucks or those monstrous station wagons of the 1960s, just like the one that my father owned. Many of these wine makers also had the equipment necessary to process the grapes and turn it into wine. Unfortunately, a few did not have the money to buy the equipment, but instead, they would borrow that from their friends after they finished with their wine-making process. A lot of Italian immigrants lived or socialized in common places or met at Italian events or feasts. This is a very nice example to understand why America is called the great melting pot of a nation.

The husband of one of my mother's cousins, a gentleman by the name of Jack, came from the northern part of Italy. He was also a partner of the family machine shop, and he would use the company pick-up truck to go and load up the grapes from the market. He had experience with the wine-making procedure since he was brought up in that part of Italy where they used to make homemade wine every year. If he liked the quality of the grapes and was able to negotiate a good price, then he would load up the truck at the market. He may not be successful on his first or second trip there due to the quality or the price being too high but, eventually, the right buying opportunity would come along. There is a four-to-six-week window when the grapes arrive almost weekly from California. Initially, the pricing would be high, but as more and more grapes start to arrive and accumulate, the wholesalers would negotiate a better price before the grapes spoil. Jack would buy maybe thirty cases and that would take two trips since each case contained thirty-six pounds of grapes and the truck would not hold more than twenty cases of them. For each case, you are expected to get between three to four gallons of wine. If we do the math, he would buy enough grapes to make at least one hundred gallons of wine. The wine had to last the whole year or until the next fall season, hopefully. But when you have that many people at the table, a gallon of wine may not be enough for each gathering. Everyone has one or two glasses of wine with dinner, and those dinners lasted for hours. One hundred gallons would just make it barely for each year. During our Saturday or Sunday gatherings, we would start eating around 3:00 PM or 4:00 PM and go well past 7:00 PM or 8:00 PM. On Saturday, it would go even later since Sunday was not a working day.

After the end of the meal, and mostly on Saturdays, while the women were busy cleaning up and making coffee together with an assortment of Italian pastries, the men would play poker or one of the other card games, which is played with Italian cards. Yes, we were also a family of gamblers in those days. But it was with quarters and dimes, not with dollar bills. The adults would put limits on the bets so that at the end of the night, your maximum loss would not be more than ten dollars or in that vicinity. I understand that in the mid-1970s, ten dollars may have been a lot for some people, but this gang could afford to lose that, notwithstanding some of the wives' complaints. Just to put everything in perspective, I believe that everyone was making over a few hundred dollars a week, which was an above-average wage then. Our cousins operated their own machine shop, so their compensation could have been even more depending on their business cycle. The same applied to my father if he was also repairing cars. This gave him an extra one hundred dollars a week. I loved observing them play; it was a magic time for me. I would sit partially next to or behind my father and observe those four or five relatives playing poker in the Italian five-card stud version. On some Saturdays, they would play past midnight, and by then, hunger became a factor again, even if they were sipping wine, brandy, or scotch all along. While the women would insist they finish their card playing and call it a night, all of a sudden, someone would say, "Let's make some fast spaghetti or warm up the leftovers." This was so diabolical because that put everything back in play. The kitchen was nice and clean and now they wanted to start all over again. When you are young and a close-knit Italian family, it is not that unrealistic to have such a request taking place. Most of the wives were accommodating, and just with their sheer number, it was not a great undertaking for their combined strength and collaboration. In no time at all, a large pan with boiling water would be ready, a couple of pounds of spaghetti, salt, and all would quickly come to fruition. There was always plenty of sauce left over, and here we are at 1:00 AM in the morning, eating again. What a wonderful and joyous life that was. Everyone eventually retired to their respective homes in the wee hours of the morning, having lived another weekend "Our Italian Way."

When it was our turn to host the weekend get-together at our home, I distinctly recall how my mother's cousins would always be surprised to find something new done to our house by my father. They used to tease my mother in her mid-thirties that she married a husband with golden hands. At times the sassier one would say to her, "What else does Giorgio have that is golden?" if you know what I mean! Their husbands ignored their comments since they were not much into staying home or doing any kind of work around the house. They had their machine shop to take care of, and, with that excuse, they were out a couple of nights a week, mostly the two twin brothers. They said they were meeting with clients after work, so they could spend some of their nights in places where they were frequent guests. I am very blessed as I look back to those days. I feel that I somewhat experienced part of what the series "Mad Men" depicted. This hour-long series portrayed on AMC TV showed what some men indulged in after hours in America during the early 1960s. I have a nostalgic feeling for that era myself, even if I was much too young. It must have been a pleasing time for businessmen where they were pretty much absolved of their behavior and decorum, which today is not at all appreciated. In their defense, they definitely did provide a very comfortable life for the family. The women played the homemaker role, while some of the men had their own gatherings in or out of the office. Obviously, all that has changed substantially today, as it should have. We will pick up some of these other wonderful times as they evolved later on.

My freshman high school year went by quickly, and now I found myself finally at the real high school in 10th grade. Suddenly, I was mixed in with the grown-up teenagers, and I had to learn this new undiscovered environment all over again. New faces and teachers and plenty of chaos ensued in that school, especially due to the critical times in America. The Vietnam War was winding down, but it already had left plenty of scars on many people, especially the older students in the junior and senior classes. Many of them had firsthand experience with the war since they witnessed some kind of loss close to their family or beloved friends. The government had instituted a lottery system to select military recruits to serve in Vietnam: "the casino draft," I called it. The older students were very weary of being drafted to serve in the military, especially if they did not attend college after their graduation. Long hair was all over the school, but my father was very strict, and I could not have hair over my ears. I wanted it, but he was very much set in his way, so I was that straight high school student. There was a civil rebellion by some of the college undergraduates against the adults, or who they called the ruling class. I observed this on TV and sometimes in listening to seniors talk about it. I observed some of this anti-society behavior, but none of my standards agreed with those demands. Most of it was wrong, and obviously, our Italian culture, and especially my parents, made sure that I was not influenced by this discourse that America was experiencing. I was sixteen now and very much up-to-date with the politics and events of those times. I would turn eighteen, and even if I was still a resident alien, I was not exempted from the draft. Anyone with a green card was eligible to be drafted into the army according to the laws of the United States.

Remember the beginning of this book when I was in Sicily on my veranda reading the newspapers about the early days of the Vietnam War and the American daily death tolls? I have now come around one hundred and eighty degrees. It now almost felt like I was part of the Vietnam War. Have you ever wondered what it would be like to be all of a sudden inside the movie that you are watching on the screen? Could I possibly be drafted in the next two years? Wow, how life sometimes takes a drastic turn, from an outsider looking in to actually being an active participant.

The high school as a whole was a wake-up call for me. I had to keep my standards, which were very traditional and definitely not with those times. My accent with the English language and not being one hundred percent confident kept me somewhat invisible to other high school students. I was working delivering local newspapers each afternoon together with that big, bulky Boston Sunday Globe on Sunday morning. My parents never believed in and actually didn't even know about, giving their kids an allowance for contributing to the household chores, as many American parents used to do and still do. It just doesn't exist in our Italian culture. You were supposed to help with the house's daily needs no matter what and, in my case, also help my father with any home repairs. It was part of your contribution to the family. It was clear to me and normal for young teenagers to work after school in order to have some spare change in their pocket. I was delivering the newspapers to the nearby homes around my neighborhood on a prescribed paper route, rain or shine, hot or cold. My social security history shows that my first contributions started in those days and have continued up to the present without ever being interrupted. I consider myself the everlasting taxpayer. Will I ever fully retire? I have been blessed to give to America because America gave me a home and a comfortable life.

It was really nice for me to have ten or fifteen dollars all the time in my pocket. It made me feel accomplished and independent at that age. The schoolwork was not a heavy burden for me; the math and sciences don't change much, no matter what country you live in. It was very fascinating, though, learning about American history and the English language in general. All considered, high school was very easy, especially once you obtained a firm understanding of the English language. It was fascinating, though, observing many high school students. The true Americans had more issues than me with some of the coursework. There was a lot of marijuana around the school grounds, and many older kids, mostly seniors, were stoned most of the time during the day. There was not much that the school administration could do about it since it was almost a way of life for those individuals. For my part, I tried to stay away from that because there were other drugs going around that were more addictive and abusive, like LSD and other hallucinogens.

Our home was located 150 feet away from the main street of the city. As you came on this main street and took a right, four houses down, you would pass a small setback brick building with a large driveway in front of it. This was the city animal hospital which faced the main street. Across, on the other side of the street, a gasoline station was situated on a large corner block. One day, I met a boy named David who was hanging around at this station, and we became friends. At night, I would stop by and talk with him. David befriended the older guy that was working at this gas station, and on some nights, he would hang around there. David would also help the gas attendant with his job, especially when too many cars would pull in all at once to fill their gas tanks. I can still envision those incredible prices at the pumps. I believe it was around thirty-five cents for a gallon, a far cry from today's prices. I eventually also ended up giving a helping hand to the working attendant that, at times, was overwhelmed with cars. It was fun to pump gas in those cars. Many of them had their tank cap just behind the back of their license plate, which folded down to allow the nozzle of the pump to be inserted to fill it. The newer cars had the side panel like you see today. Boy, did it take a lot of gasoline to fill them! The 1970s were known for those big eight-cylinder engines, the notorious V8. The muscle car era, as we call it now. Older teenagers used to drive around in some of these, like the Plymouth Hemi Superbird or the Barracuda, the Pontiac Firebird or the Trans Am, the Chevrolet Chevelle, or the Oldsmobile 442. All of these cars are highly sought after today, and some of them are worth twenty or thirty times what they sold for in the 1970s. When some of these cars left the gas station, those young drivers would step down on the gas, and the tires would spin, and the sound of the screeching rubber and the smell of the overheated rubber would be left behind. All great memories.

I always wanted to own a car that could do that, but I would have to wait many decades to get that M series BMW that I actually do own today. "Life is a bitch," is what people tell me. Responsibilities, the true realities, and the kids were a first priority. That dream had to be put on hold. But I am not bitter at all and don't have many regrets; it was a nice run. As you read on, I will dedicate a few pages to it as we go through this last part of my book. Let me warn you that the fast life of America did take me for a nice ride with many accomplishments but also with a few regrets. I would do it all over again if I had the opportunity. Maybe I might have slowed it down a little bit and paid a little more attention to some of the things that I may have rushed through. Maybe I should have spent a little bit more time to smell the roses and enjoy the coffee.

Getting back to my new friend David, he was the son of a second-generation Irish immigrant of the early 1900s. He told me that most afternoons after school, he worked at the animal hospital, right across the street from the gas station. He also said that he lived on the first street to the left of it, about five houses down, and I told him that I lived on the right of it, about three houses down. Wow, what a coincidence that we were also close neighbors! He worked at the animal hospital for about four hours each afternoon, but sometimes he would also go back at night for a couple of hours. The doctor needed help when the clients brought in their pets to hold them or to assist him with other tasks.

His parents, like mine, were also very strict. He was attending high school at a private Catholic high school in our city, the same grade as me. I remembered hearing of this particular high school from my mother's cousins. They mentioned it to my parents as a possible place for me to be enrolled after I graduated 8th grade. But with my bad experience at that elementary Catholic school, they opted for the city's public school. "Thanks, Mom and Dad!" In actuality, the public high school was not as good as the private school that David was attending, but it was a far cry from that decrepit elementary school that I wasted over two years attending.

David said that the veterinarian was looking to hire someone else because he was very busy, especially during his nightly visits. Additionally, he wanted to give David a couple of afternoons off so he could do his homework. Well, he brought me to see the doctor the following week for a short interview. The doctor, a full-fledged experienced veterinarian, lived in a large one-family home with his wife and mother-in-law right next to this standalone building, just a few steps away. This doctor was probably in his mid-fifties, a Second World War Polish Jewish immigrant. He was pretty distinctive looking, and I felt during the interview that he liked to be with younger bright teenagers. The job was not for the faint-hearted. He had a kennel room with about thirty cages of different sizes that needed to be cleaned each morning and afternoon. In the morning, he had an older man that worked there while we were in school. This older man would go home at 3:00 PM, and my job was to relieve him just like David did each afternoon when he worked.

He introduced me to him, and during my interview, he told me that he would also be training me on all the work that had to be done. This work included cleaning all the cages again after the initial morning cleaning and continuing on with any other work that had to be done. The kennel also had a door to an enclosed cemented outside yard to release the dogs for their exercise while their cages were cleaned. The job also required me to bathe the dogs and comb them out if a client brought in their pet in the morning for that purpose. The doctor would train me with the correct techniques to accomplish these tasks. I was very much interested in getting this job, even if I had to clean dog poop, spray the cages with a cleaner, put fresh newspapers on their base, and mop the floors. I thought that I was ready for a real job now and that, eventually, there would be some kind of an upside to it. The newspaper job was no longer for me. I was becoming an adult, and even if I had to clean the animal mess and mop the floors, for me, it was a promotion. After my tour and interview, the doctor said that I could start the next day and begin learning the job requirements. The pay was much better than delivering newspapers, and I would be working indoors and not outside in the elements. The vicinity of my home was perfect, and I was sure that my parents would like me to work for a doctor. This job led to a long and close relationship with my friend, David, and also with the veterinarian whom I believe was named "Harold."

My father, in the meantime, was advancing in his profession very quickly. He landed yet another new job with a bigger trucking company just outside of Boston. His job description was the same: reconditioning the old diesel engines from the trucks and reinstalling them. The pay grade was even better, and the hours were perfect; he would be home shortly after 4:00 PM without having to work any overtime. He said that it was not worth working those extra hours because, at the end of the week, the government would penalize him by taking out too much in taxes and other contributions. He also wanted to be home early so that he could do his own independent mechanic work and have the time to continue updating our home.

I can still remember when he decided to dig a trench almost two feet deep all around the home's foundation. Our old basement leaked during the snow-melting season. The water would infiltrate inside through the old dry-stone basement construction. The project for that year was to erect and pour a cement wall all around the foundation in order to stop water infiltration. We dug a one-foot trench below the foundation and poured cement to erect a wall about one foot thick and one foot over the current base. My father had gravel delivered by a large truck and dumped in the driveway together with construction sand. He also purchased many bags of cement to prepare the mix for the construction of this retaining wall. If you care to know, guess who was the person who took turns with him mixing and pouring this cement wall? Yes, it was I, the eldest son and the only one that, at the age of seventeen, could endure this physically demanding task. This was good old-fashioned laborer work, where you would develop calluses on your hands if you failed to wear gloves.

This work went on for the entire spring and part of the summer, a piece of the wall at a time as the weather permitted. It was finished by early fall, before any early snow. I can still feel my back and arms hurting when I think about that project. My father was in his early forties and had learned this trade from watching and helping his own father, Giuseppe, who was known for building homes in Tripoli. This kind of work, mixing cement with sand and gravel and pouring it into a framework, is not for everyone. I cannot imagine if I had to do it for the rest of my life as my everyday work. I must say, though, that I was in the best shape of my life, having sweated so much on that job with him. He taught me how to manually mix the cement and how to pour it behind that temporary prefabricated wooden form, much like today's home foundation construction. Thanks, Dad, for giving me the opportunity of working with you hand in hand when I was a teenager. That work with my father was very demanding and not for the fainthearted, but it built mutual respect at the same time.

I did not get encouraging praise such as "Well done, Son," handshakes, or pats on my back; my father did not express himself that way. He hardly expressed those feelings; maybe it was because his mother died when he was very young, and he was never exposed to those motherly consolations or warm motherly interactions. My other take was that he saw the destruction and miseries of the Second World War when he was only thirteen. I listened to those conversations with his friends. He would recount living at a boys' colony, where his father sent him in Italy since the Fascist government wanted to protect their young men during the African war. The deal was that the war was going to be fought only in Africa and would never reach the Italian homeland. But instead, the Allied forces pushed the Axis forces out of Africa. They advanced first into southern Italy and then into Northern Italy, driving the Germans out and defeating the Fascists along the way. The war quickly reached even those secured Italian boys' colonies and all of a sudden, they were on their own, looking for food and their own protection. Many times, he described looking up at the sky from the boys' colony and watching American planes flying overhead, ready to release their bombs in the nearby towns next to their camp and obscuring the sun as they flew by. Food was very scarce, and they had to steal it from the local farmers, who also had very little to share. During our family gatherings, these war experiences were always at the forefront and vivid among everyone there. We talked about those events, but we always acknowledged that we were lucky to be in America, living in the most powerful country in the world. Those times hardened his character because there was nobody around to give him a tap on his shoulder or a compliment; there was no time for that. All of that work made me aware of what it takes to have a home and maintain a home, but also how hard it is to be a construction worker.

Those three years of high school were a wonderful time for me. I had a great job at the animal hospital, money in my pocket, and I was finally on my way to adulthood. During the summer of 1974, the whole family was able to travel to Italy for approximately one month for a real earned vacation. My father took care of all the family expenses while my mother saved for this trip using the funds from her part-time job. In our Italian culture, there is no "my part" or "your part." We all contributed as a family to the benefit of everyone.

We flew business class on the glamorous Pan Am airline of the times, direct to Rome from Boston. Those were the days when airline travel was a seamless, even luxurious, experience. I fondly recall the meals offered on the plane. The airlines, particularly the international carriers, made you feel like you were dining at a five-star restaurant. I believe that my father wanted us to realize what we were not able to see during our time in Messina. I could also speculate that maybe he wanted to prove to us that he had made the right choice to immigrate to America and that this vacation was a small piece of that initial American dream.

When we arrived in Italy, we traveled to places where he stayed during his teenage years during the war. The boys' colony in the northern part of Italy facing the Adriatic Sea was now converted to a lovely beach and country resort with many pine trees extending all the way to the sandy beach. When we arrived at this hotel, he was curious about what the inside looked like since he stayed there for many months as a boy. He and the other boys used to walk the barren beach by the seaside, which now contained many umbrellas and chairs elegantly placed on the sand. This visit was symbolic for my father because not many people were given the opportunity to revisit and relive places and times that were part of their lives.

We traveled up the northeastern coast of Italy, visiting many beautiful places like San Marino, which is the smallest republic in the world. Then we moved up the coast and stopped in Rimini, Venice, and our final stop, Trieste, on the Yugoslavian border. We were able to enter Yugoslavia with a twenty-hour visitor's pass granted to Italian citizens. At the time, Josip Broz Tito, a communist revolutionary and statesman, was president. Tito served in various positions in the Yugoslavian government from 1943 until his death in 1980. Why my father ventured there, I will never know. Maybe he wanted to show us the contrast between Italy and communist Yugoslavia. My father was always firing on all cylinders and once said to me, "I respect a person that has traveled the world more than a university grad."

We drove across to the west coast of Italy for a five-day visit to some well-known and culturally affluent cities, like Florence, Pisa, Viareggio, and the coast of Liguria. We then moved south for a couple of days in Rome: "The Eternal City" with its breathtaking historical attractions. "Wow," I said to myself, "we lived in Italy for almost ten years, and we were not able to visit any of these beautiful places that I studied while I was in school in Messina. Maybe he really is trying to prove his point of why we immigrated to America." Now here we were with plenty of time and money to finally learn about Italy by immersing ourselves in the attractions that we had only read about. I ask myself now: "Was this part of his way to show us what can be accomplished if you work hard in America?" Who knows? I believe that my father looked at his actions more than his words, and maybe those actions and experiences did speak louder than words. Sometimes I wish that I could still talk to him to discuss those times and others that await us in the following pages.

After a couple of days, we were finally heading toward Sicily, where we planned to spend almost ten days before we would travel back to the United States. As we headed south, we briefly stopped in beautiful Naples and the surrounding coastal cities like Sorrento and Amalfi. One afternoon, we walked the excavated ruins of Pompeii, which brought back memories from my Italian history classes. What also stood out as we traveled around Italy was the cuisine. Every region that we visited had its own unique cuisine that awakened our senses. Since we had no money to travel while living in Sicily, we could only imagine how delicious the food was. But, thanks to my father, with a couple of extra dollars in his pocket, he was really able to give us the experience to finally taste many of those dishes that had eluded us.

As we headed toward Sicily, everyone was excited to finally see our old mother city. We crossed that beautiful Strait of Messina that separates mainland Italy from the island of Sicily in one of the ships that you drive on with your car. When we finally landed in Messina, we were reunited with my Aunt Anna and were her guests in her large apartment near the center of the city. It was a bittersweet reunion. We were all grown up, as it had been over six years since we left on that large ocean liner to find our way to America. My parents had a lot to talk about and share about those initial years in America. Just the fact that we were able to afford this visit to Italy spoke multitudes about our accomplishments in Boston. Life in Messina was still the same; nothing really changed there. I was able to personally assert that our American life was so much more dynamic and productive. Yes, everyone worked every day, and so did my father in Messina. However, we were able to accomplish a lot more as a result of our focus, resolutions, and opportunities in America. We already owned our home in Boston, which we could not afford to do in nine years in Italy. We also had a large and fairly new car in America. Yes, in Messina, we also owned a car, but we could just barely fit in it. We were able to afford many additional comforts in America without worrying about making ends meet. That American weekly paycheck was able to provide visibility into the future, unlike that dreaded monthly salary that my parents had to watch every penny of in order for it to last every month.

We finally visited our old neighborhood, and our apartment was now rented to a nice family there. Well, wait a moment! Rented? How can that be? During the last six years, the Italian government offered those apartments for sale to whoever was able to buy them. Well, my father was able to buy our old apartment from the Italian government for only $ 2,000.00. The discount was because the government gave everyone credit for all the years that they paid rent. So, after being government renters, we were now the actual owners of our small apartment in Messina while we lived and owned our home in Boston. What an accomplishment in those six short years! The American way of life was alive and well, with much more to come.

During the last few days of our visit, I was able to spend time with my old friends that still lived in our condominium complex. A couple of them just came back from military service in Italy, and since I was the youngest one, they had so much more life experience. But guess what? They wanted to find out only about me and my American life. Question after question, what are you doing? Do you have one of those beautiful American girlfriends that we see on Italian TV? What about a car, do you drive one of those big fancy cars? They wanted to hear me speaking English; they loved the sound of our language. I could tell that everyone was struggling in their youth. Jobs were hard to come by, and money was still not that easy to earn. Some of them, being almost twenty years old, still depended on their parents for financial help. In the United States, I was attending college and working at the same time. My American life was a dream for them. I invited them out to places like a pizza restaurant or other dancing spots in the city. I was willing to pay for everything, but they did not allow me to do that. They said that I was their guest and in Italy, you are not allowed to pay. I could see how they all struggled to put their money together to make sure the bill was covered. They said to me, "When we come to America, you can pay for us then," but I knew that would never happen. My father was right: if we had stayed in

Italy, I probably would have struggled just like them to find economic freedom, work, and independence. I think that our trip back to the homeland was a reality check for me. I realized how I was so much better off than my friends that I left behind many years ago.

When I finally arrived back in Boston, I was even more appreciative of my life in America. That sense of accomplishment drove me even more to concentrate and move forward as much as I could. Shortly after that, I graduated from a local community college, and I was hired by a well-known doctor who was the head of the Department of Nuclear Medicine at Boston University Medical Center. I had simultaneously attended a college program of studies that this doctor created by securing a federal grant at the community college. If you could get the federal government via the Department of Education to establish these programs, it said a lot about this doctor's political connections in Washington D.C. during the early 1970s. This program required each student to spend a minimum of 1,000 hours in an internship with an affiliated hospital. It also required you to take a curriculum that included some pre-med courses such as Anatomy and Physiology, Biochemistry, Radiation Physics, and Statistics. In the summers, I did my internship full-time at various affiliated hospitals, but I was lucky to spend most of those months at this doctor's hospital.

Toward the end of my internship, he said to me, "When you finish your requirements and graduate, don't go look for a job!" "Why?" I asked him. He responded, "Because you will be working here for me." I said, "Doctor, there is no job opening in your department." "Don't worry, Joe," he said. "I will write you a check for your work every week from my own personal checking account, and you will be hired by the hospital soon enough." Well, that was exactly what happened within ninety days of him paying me out of his own pocket every week: I was hired by that hospital as a member of the Nuclear Medicine technology staff. At that time, I was the only one in that department that passed the test to be a registered and certified Nuclear Medicine professional. I also was a member of "The Society of Nuclear Medicine."

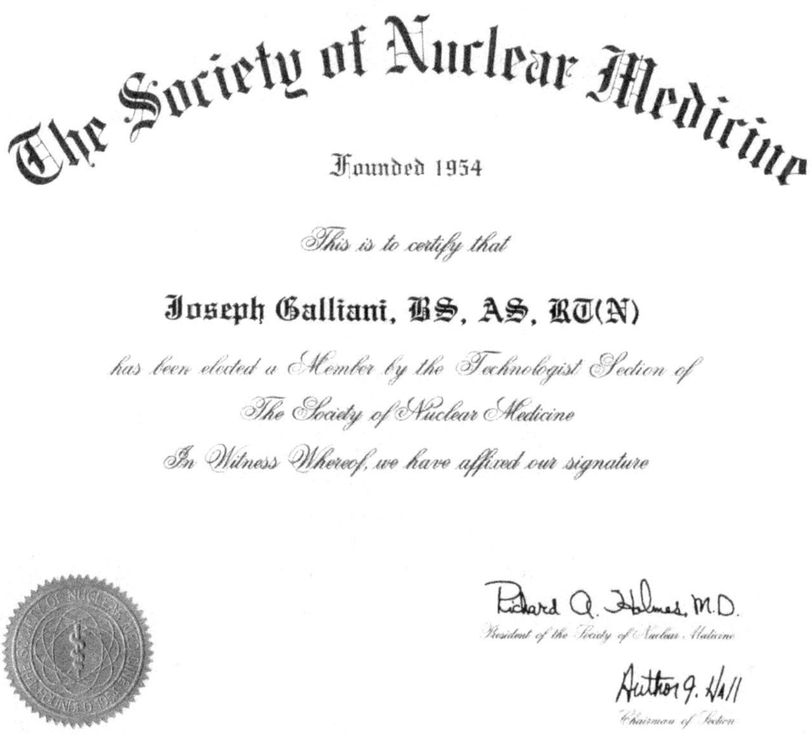

The Society of Nuclear Medicine

Founded 1954

This is to certify that

Joseph Galliani, BS, AS, RT(N)

has been elected a Member by the Technologist Section of

The Society of Nuclear Medicine

In Witness Whereof, we have affixed our signature

President of the Society of Nuclear Medicine

Chairman of Section

Certificate of membership in the Society of Nuclear Medicine.

This was my first great victory right out of college. I started working for this great man who was later referred to, and is known in history, as one of the "Fathers of Nuclear Medicine." The guy was a gentleman in every sense of the word. I never saw him upset in the seven years that I worked for him. He always had a smile on his face as he made his way to the department every afternoon. This doctor put me in for back pay for all the weeks that I had been working for him (don't ask me how he did it), and I proudly reimbursed him for all of his weekly check advances when I received that initial large check from the hospital.

I also found out during my initial months there that he had been the chief of nuclear medicine also at the VA hospital in Boston for over twenty years. I guess that explains his connection with the federal government and his establishment of the nuclear medicine curriculum at the college. This hospital position allowed me to learn what I really loved and wanted to do with my life. It was not going to be medical school. I was into technology more than medicine.

In the late 1970s and early 1980s, the nuclear medicine department was the only place where you would find a powerful computer. Those were the days of a major American powerhouse in the computer industry called "Digital Equipment Corporation." Their powerful mini-computers were called PDP 11 and Vax Supermini. Their processors and architecture allowed it to run FORTRAN and other programming languages. The mini-computer that we purchased for our nuclear medicine department was used for our digital imaging system and ran mostly on a FORTRAN software package designed for our gamma cameras. The doctor that hired me saw my interest in knowing more about that computer technology as time progressed. He said to me, "Joseph, go to Boston University and take all the computer courses that you like after work. I will have the hospital pay for them." I had such a great job! I was well-paid and had access to a free university education that eventually catapulted me to my final line of work.

Within one year of working at the hospital, I was able to buy my first new car.

Me in my early twenties with my first brand-new car.

I was making a great salary, was well-liked by my peers, and was further advancing myself in the technology sector, all by being financially independent. But even with that, I never thought about moving out of my father's home. There was just too much family in me, and I had to live it; it was just part of my upbringing and culture. Many young men in those days, when they finally had a job, would move on and live on their own and sometimes be far away from their families. My Italian family never once, or even remotely, thought to bring up that option. I had the independence that I needed as a young man and was glad to still live in my father's home. If you live the American dream, everyone should be a part of and enjoy those accomplishments. My personal achievements paired with those of my father.

Two years earlier, he secured a new job, and this would be the last company that he worked for until he finally retired. They provided ready-to-pour concrete for major construction projects in Boston. The company was, and still is, located in a well-known Boston neighborhood called Charlestown, which is home to the USS Constitution and the Bunker Hill Monument. This company eventually became one of the largest suppliers of concrete in southern New England. He was hired as a master diesel engine mechanic. But his job was very special. He worked mostly alone in a large room with a big overhead door. This opening allowed a large backhoe to deliver large broken diesel engines that were dismounted from one of the concrete trucks in order to be totally rebuilt by my father. He had maybe five newly re-built engines on one side of the room that were ready to be picked up to replace the broken one just delivered. The broken engine would be dropped on the opposite side of the room, where he also had many more in different stages of the re-building process. At that time, the company owned about eighty concrete mixer trucks; they now have over 250. My father's job was really easygoing. As long as he had new engines ready to go, there was no pressure, and he always kept up with them. Each engine could take a month or more to be completed, but if parts were back-ordered, it would take much longer. But my father just moved on to another one that did not require a part that was unavailable. I remember that I used to visit him during the work day, if I had a couple of hours of spare time. I would drive my car right in front of that large overhead door, get out, and look through the small glass windows on that door to see if he was there. I would knock on the windows if he was squatted down behind those big engines so he could see me. Most of the time if he was there, he would open the door and let me in. I was wearing nice clothes, because of my job and he used to warn me, "Watch out! Don't get too close or touch those dirty, broken engines on that side of the room." The room was part of a larger hanger that was probably sixty feet long by at least thirty feet wide. It was separated from the main shop, but it had a small side door which he kept closed for privacy and not to hear the truck noises.

That was a gateway to a much larger drive-in garage used for the trucks to be driven inside and serviced for all kinds of other mechanical repairs. There were maybe ten to twelve other mechanics working there doing different maintenance services to trucks that were temporarily taken off their route. Some of those services included changing the engine or transmission oil, replacing antifreeze, brakes, or tires, and other repairs. These were short services that took maybe a couple of days, unlike what my father did, which used to take much longer.

My father was really not supervised by anyone at his new job, probably because the management team actually had no clue what he was doing. They would just go to his work area to see him, but mostly to let him know that his parts had arrived for any of the engines he was rebuilding. Those parts were very expensive and probably cost thousands of dollars depending on what the repairs required. Some engines had a cracked main body and needed to be disposed of. A new unit or engine block would be ordered and then all of the new parts would be assembled inside by my father. The other mechanics would pick up one of my father's newly re-built engines with the backhoe when it was ready. They would bring it to the main garage and install it in the truck where the old broken one was taken out. When everything was ready to go, they would let my father know because they wanted him to be there to turn on that new engine. I would have done the same if I were them because each engine was worth over twenty-five thousand dollars. The shop mechanics did not want to take any responsibility if they did something wrong and broke that new engine right from the start. As the story goes, my father would schedule a time frame and get on top of the truck to make sure that they connected everything correctly. He would also check the electrical system to ensure that all was in working order. Finally, he would check that all the engine fluids were full as specified and everything was tightly torqued.

Only then would he get inside the truck cabin, make sure all the indicators and lights came on, and only then crank that engine on.

Lo and behold, a plume of black smoke would escape from the exhaust system, and the engine would start with a mighty roar, ready to go to work again. He would tell everyone not to race the engine above a particular range until the engine had passed so many hours of operation. He would speak with the manager of the shop to contact the drivers that were assigned to drive that truck to make sure not to race the engine above a particular range for at least a week of operation. The mechanics observing that the engine started on that first crank would applaud and cheer for another job well done. History was repeating itself almost the same as the mechanics did at the Rodriquez Company in Messina. I am sure that many of them wondered, "How does this guy do it?" He is closed in his own room, he puts every part back in place just like the original manufacturer and then he turns the key of the engine, and it starts on the first turn all the time. If they only knew that my father worked on much bigger and more advanced engines at the hydrofoil shipyard in Italy a decade ago, but they had no clue.

As soon as 4:00 PM came, my father packed up his personal belongings and went home. He didn't want to hear anything about overtime unless things went very wrong that day. He wanted no part in staying there, not even one minute longer, even if he would get paid time and a half per hour. He was absolutely right: he was getting paid well for his skills, the company was up and always running at one hundred percent and making money "hands over fists." As he used to say to me: "I am an hourly worker, and my earnings get taxed by the tax code to the penny. The corporation has its own way of lowering its taxes. Instead of paying those additional taxes on their profits, they would instead buy new trucks and other equipment. They get bigger and more profitable with that investment. It is the American way for big corporations to grow and reinvest their profits to enhance their business, being more productive and hiring more employees, capitalism at its best."

It was during that year that my father was asked by his old friend, Antonio, living in Italy, if he was interested in buying an apartment in the building where he lived. If you recall from my "Out of Africa" part of the book, both of them started a small repair business in the late 1950s in Tripoli. Unfortunately, the course of events separated them, and they both went back to Italy, but they always kept in touch via mail. Antonio settled in the northern portion of Italy in a very historic city called Verona. This city is best known as the setting of the love story of Romeo and Juliet. The city is also known as Little Rome, where a great Roman Arena called the "Arena of Verona" is located. Large-scale opera performances are given there. The city is one of the most popular and beautiful cities in Italy and includes a fashion district attracting many of the country's aristocrats and tourists. Antonio had opened a leather purse and accessories store in the fashion district and was doing quite well. This was a far cry from fixing and repairing cars and trucks in Tripoli with my father. Antonio and my father would talk on the phone every few months to see how everyone was doing in their respective countries.

The real estate opportunity was priced very aggressively by the deceased owner's son. Antonio told him that he would take care of the apartment by renting it out and attending to any repairs needed. Let's not forget that my father purchased our small apartment in Messina several years earlier, and it was also rented. This second real estate opportunity came at the perfect time when the American Dollar was very strong against the Italian Lira. The apartment was much larger than the one in Messina, in a more elegant and well-known Northern city. My parents always put money away every week and accumulated some cash in the bank. I believe the cost of that apartment translated to $15,000.00 when converted to Italian currency. The building where the apartment was located was built in the last ten years, which was practically new by Italian standards.

I will stop here to address a question that my readers may have at this point. Why is my father looking to buy real estate in Italy and not in America, where he was living? Everyone should know that my father always thought then that when he would retire in thirty years or so, that he would go back to Italy and live an easy life in his home country. Oh boy, did he get that all so wrong, as we will find out in the upcoming ending of this book.

But notwithstanding the distance, cost, and other factors, my father liked the opportunity to own a nice apartment in one of the best cities in Italy. My mother also agreed that having a nice apartment in Verona would be a great investment, especially once we sell the one in Messina. They ended up purchasing the apartment for much less than they initially thought. The owner lowered the price by $1,000.00, and the Italian lira lost even more value against the dollar in the next three months, lowering the total cost by an extra $500.00. My parents were now the proud owners of three homes; one in Boston, where we lived, and now two others in Italy. If that is not the American dream, I don't know what else to call it. This was all done with hard work and perseverance. He would be at work by 7:00 AM and leave at 4:00 PM, while my mother worked part-time from 8:00 AM until 2:00 PM, also five days a week. As I mentioned, my father would also work on neighbors' or friends' cars on some Saturdays or Sundays. These extra dollars earned all added up in the long run.

The next summer, our family planned a second trip to Italy. Everyone wanted to see that new apartment. Even if the unit was already rented to a young couple, we would meet them and ask them to see it. This trip would only be three weeks instead of a month like the previous one. We would stay one week with Antonio since his apartment was a large two-bedroom, with two bathrooms plus an extra study room. His only daughter was not living at home because she was attending a nearby college in Milan. My father decided to stay at his house instead for only two days. On the other days, we reserved a suite at a nearby hotel on the Lake of Garda, a few miles from Verona. Today, this lake is a very expensive and exclusive place to live and visit, frequented by the rich and famous. This lake is where my father was dispatched many years earlier to service the hydrofoils that provide water connectivity between vital tourist spots. You may recall in our "Out of Italy" section when I covered his work away from Messina. Life has a strange way of working its way back to remind you of the past, the work that you did, and how your life has changed.

For my part, I was also able to get three weeks' vacation from the hospital. Now in my twenties, I would not miss this trip for anything. I also wanted to see that part of Italy where the new apartment was located and what the surrounding vicinities offered. I was also very much interested in traveling back to Messina for our last two weeks. When we arrived in Verona, which none of us had ever visited before, it was like a breath of fresh air right from the start! The city was so clean, vibrant, and full of historic structures.

We reached Antonio's building, rang his apartment number, and waited for the building access door to open. Then, out of the blue, we heard someone loudly saying from a balcony, maybe on the third floor above us in Italian, "Well, it is about time that you came and see me." That was Antonio telling my father in his own way: "Welcome." The door opened remotely and as the elevator door opened, there was Antonio. I never met him personally, but I knew much about his past history and relationship with my father. He was a slender petite man, maybe in his late forties, well-groomed, sport shirt and dress pants. I saw him and my father hugging and actually holding each other for a while. What a chilling and beautiful vision that was. Obviously, everyone had aged much, from men in their twenties to mature men in their forties. Antonio also hugged my mother and told her that she hadn't changed much. She introduced me, my sister, and my brother. Antonio said, "Giorgio, you did well. Look at your son. He is a man, and your daughter reminds me of my daughter, your young son Vincenzo he looks just like his grandfather in Tripoli. Come on, let's go upstairs. My wife is waiting." I was so impressed by how clean the building was kept as we walked the short corridor on the third floor that led to his apartment. As we approached his condo, he pointed thirty feet down the hallway "Your apartment is the last unit on this floor." Wow, I thought to myself, what a classy entrance. I couldn't wait to see his apartment. Hopefully, it would be similar to the one that my father bought.

As we entered his apartment, we were greeted by his wife, a kind, attractive woman, maybe a few years younger than Antonio, smiling and hugging all of us, welcoming us to their home. Their apartment was so spacious, with high ceilings, bright, and with ceramic floors everywhere. A brief tour really astonished me; it was a far cry from our apartment in Messina. This new construction projected well, and the rooms were well-placed and flowed seamlessly. The kitchen and the bathrooms were impeccably finished, with marble floors, state-of-the-art cabinets, toilets, a bidet, plus fancy sinks with well-designed accessories. Everyone was so interested in finding out about each other's lives and what it was like living in America, but my father was also very interested in Antonio's newfound line of work. We had a delicious dinner prepared by his wife. Antonio said that tomorrow around lunch time my father's tenants had agreed to let us see our apartment. I was so curious to find out how it compared to Antonio's apartment, but he told us that it was pretty much the same size and some of the finishes were slightly different, but overall, we would like it.

The next day we were able to meet my father's new tenants. They were a young professional married couple, and the wife was expecting their first child. As Antonio said, the apartment was very nice, spacious, and also full of light since it was a corner unit. My father really hit a home run with this purchase. We left their leased apartment after twenty minutes and wished everyone well. During the afternoon, we visited Antonio's leather store; his wife was there earlier in the morning to open it. I was amazed to see the location of this store right in the street where thirty or forty other stores were located, selling all kinds of fashion apparel. This street was well known in the city as the fashion district. The store was full of all kinds of women's and men's handbags since, in those days, it was fashionable for men to carry a small hand-held purse for their documents, cigarettes, papers, etc. It was evident that he was very successful selling his merchandise; in just the thirty minutes that we were there, several people came in, and they all bought something.

Just before dinner one evening, Antonio's brother-in-law, Marco, came to visit. After we all got acquainted with this young man in his late twenties, he then turned around and said to me, "Tonight we are going out on the nearby Lake of Garda discotheque, and your sister can also join us." My parents became a little apprehensive, but I stood my ground, and my sister said, "I am going with them also." It seemed that night life in that part of Italy didn't start until late, with some of the night clubs not even opening until 11:00 PM. Obviously, I was very familiar with the nightclub scene because, in Boston, I would not miss many weekends at my favorite night spots. My sister was a different story; my parents were very protective of her, so I had to cover for her all the time. But now the rabbit was out of the hat, as we say. My parents could not be that assertive in order not to look too old-fashioned. We went out around 10:00 PM, which was later than what I was used to. We drove to the lake shores, about twenty minutes away, along a beautiful winding road in Marco's small sports car of that era, a luxurious Lancia HP. Not many young men could afford such a car, but this was the Verona life.

Our new-found friend knew all the spots. That must have been part of his bachelor life but as we were driving, he told us that he actually had a girlfriend. I believe that he took this opportunity of us being there to bring us to some of his old night spots. "Wait until we get to this discotheque," he said. "It is usually full of people, but if there is nothing going on there, we will drive to a different one just five minutes away."

My sister was already in heaven when we pulled up to this first place next to the lake shore. When we parked the car, the lot was already crowded. We could also hear the music from there. This was very different for me also since I never went to a nightclub by the water in Boston. My sister was in ecstasy. As we entered the club, Marco knew the bouncers. They actually said, "Hey Marco, where have you been? We haven't seen you in a while." He replied, "Well, you know, my girlfriend doesn't like to go out much." They said, "Well, bring her here next time. She will love it." But he said, "I don't think so with all the girls here, she gets jealous." The guy said, "Don't worry, she will love you even more after, or else the girls here will steal you from her. By the way, who are your two friends?" Marco replied, "They are personal friends of my older sister. They are Italian, but they live in America, and they are visiting us." The doorman changed his demeanor, suddenly saying, "Hey, Americano, welcome to our club. I am sure it is nothing like America, but this is all we can do." He directed us to go inside and enjoy the music.

This place was pretty nice, actually. There was an inside club and then a large outside garden with music, lights, and a nice outdoor seating area. There were two dance floors: one inside and one outside. Many people were there, but Marco said, "Wait one more hour; you will not be able to walk around. It gets very crowded." He also met a few of his friends that were there. We had a great time dancing, meeting, and talking to many people. My sister had a ball since some of the men liked her, especially when they found out she was an American there on vacation. I also met some beautiful and interesting women, but that would be just a one-time meeting. There were no cell phones then, no texting, and no WhatsApp. You needed to live there, or else there would be no next time.

We stayed there until 1:00 AM. Thank God that Marco's sister gave me the building keys so we could quietly get inside, go to the spare room, and sleep. We ventured out again with Marco two days later before we left Verona. This other nightclub was even better than the first one: bigger with a very upscale crowd. I said to myself, "Wow, I should come here every summer since we now have the apartment here. Maybe it is my destiny to come back to Italy." Unfortunately, none of that ever happened. There just were not enough opportunities to take me away from my comfortable and beautiful life in America. My parents would be back in Verona but not with me. I had things going on in Boston that became more important than starting a new life in Italy.

We finally said goodbye to everybody, but my parents said, "We will see you next year." It was a ten-hour car drive to Sicily and our old home city of Messina. This time Aunt Anna was living in a beautiful spacious villa leased from the government. Uncle Franco was now a dignitary as the head of the military recruiting office in Messina. The villa also had a little side apartment attached to the back side where we all stayed. The villa was a standalone single-family home located in a high point of the city with beautiful views of the Strait of Messina from the large garden. It had gate access at the perimeter, which was always locked, so it was pretty secure.

What really stands out in my mind from those two weeks of summer in Sicily was what unexpectedly awaited us. Uncle Franco had been working on a great project for the last five years during the summer months in Messina. You may remember his father from the "Out of Italy" part of this book. He was the Port Master in Messina when we immigrated to America on that luxury ocean liner. He had since retired and was able to secure a long-term lease of an empty beachfront property from the Italian government. He already owned his own private land 300 feet from this particular strip of the beach; the government also gave him the right to improve the beachfront within certain limits. This location on the outskirts of Messina was highly desirable during the summer for its beautiful sandy beach and crystal-clear water. He built a partially removable strip of small summer cabins together with some fixed supporting infrastructure around them. In Italy, these complexes are called "Beach Lidos." A Lido is a small waterfront resort on the beach that does not incorporate any overnight rooms like a hotel would. The complex is usually built with small, attached cabins, maybe six feet by ten or twelve feet. These cabins have electric service but only for a small refrigerator, a lamp, or a radio. You would use this space to change into your bathing suit, hang your clothing, and store food or beverages that you brought with you. The complex, depending on the beachfront space, could have fifty or one hundred or more of these structures. Local beach-goers could rent them by the week, month, or the whole summer season. Lidos often contain a freshwater shower and a small bar with food and drinks available. Many of them also have entertainment plus activities during the day and early night. My uncle's lido was a beautiful summer dream for me and my sister to spend almost every single day of our two weeks vacation there. It was paradise. There were about one hundred cabins right on the sand with a beverage bar and fresh sandwiches. He had a jukebox and a couple of pinball machines together with a foosball table. Most of the people that rented these cabins paid for the whole summer season; it was a place to gather with friends and meet new friends. Most of them would arrive early in the morning, especially on weekends, and many would leave late at night. When we first arrived there with my cousin Maria, now a teenager and the only daughter of Franco, I could not believe my uncle's setup. He had thought of everything, including a large deck that surrounded all of the cabins and umbrellas for anyone to use. Everyone could gather there with tables and chairs that he placed around the edges of this large deck. Additionally, each cabin had a small space right in front of it; some guests would relax on their chairs right in front of their cabin. Everything and everyone was less than one hundred feet from the beautiful sandy beach and the clear green-blue colored Tyrrhenian Sea.

When we arrived, my niece and my uncle introduced us to many guests that they knew well. The usual introduction was, "These are my nephew and niece; they live in America and are our guests with their parents for a couple of weeks." I felt like a VIP in those surroundings and to make things even more incredible, many young beautiful Italian teenage girls were there with their parents and friends. Well, was this a place made in heaven or what? I would never have imagined a more pleasurable and viable vacation in my wildest dreams. Every morning, if possible, I would try to go with my uncle to his lido. This property was the last one in a row of five or six other similar ones built earlier. When you arrived there, you were in heaven. It felt like you were on a private island. On the third day that we got there, as I moved around the lido, I was pleasantly surprised to see a couple of my old friends there. We all hugged each other; five long years had elapsed since our last meeting. Not to mention all of the new friends that my cousin introduced us to made it a great two weeks of summer in Sicily. That experience is still fresh in my memory. I was a young man then, and I couldn't have asked for more. Those organized night dances with extremely beautiful young girls, the swimming contests with all the other young men, and those couple of very touching moments by the beach under the stars were memorable.

Me at my uncle's beach lido complex in the late 1970s.

Sometimes I wish that I had stayed behind and forgot about going back. But, I had to continue my American dream, where my life was now in my new homeland. Did I make the right decision? Absolutely. It was just a taste of summer life in Sicily; there were three other seasons to contend with that were not for the beach. But now I live in Florida and every day is a potential beach day. When I was not yet a full-time resident, I used to fly in every month since my son, Giorgio - yes, named after my father - was attending college there. He used to greet me at the West Palm Beach airport every time I flew in with a kiss, a hug, and then that wonderful phrase, "Welcome back to paradise, Papa." He decided after he graduated to remain in Florida and make it his home; he is thriving and enjoying every minute of it with his young wife.

When we all came back to reality, our home in America, it was back to work, accomplishments, and family. The 1980s were here, but before they arrived, my sister, Alba, got married after a brief engagement. She was attending hairdressing school and working at a salon where she met a young man, also an Italian immigrant. They fell in love, and the rest is history. They rented a nice apartment nearby our home, and we could still see each other at least a couple of times a week. Our household was now smaller, but those extended family parties kept on going, and we would spend the holidays at each other's homes.

In 1983, an event that would change my life forever happened. It was compounded by many other related occurrences, but there was one that clinched it all. The chief physician of nuclear medicine was retiring, and I lost my only reason to remain in that line of work. I knew at that point that I would not continue with any additional education in the medical field. I just did not have it in me; I could never be a good doctor. I learned in those six or seven years working in the Department of Nuclear Medicine, wearing all kinds of hats, that I did not like what I had experienced and seen. I witnessed too many of my patients dying and that left me feeling depressed and powerless, not something I wanted to take home every day. Additionally, because of my senior status, I was looking more deeply into the history of my patients. I was not taking any tests ordered by the doctors for granted! I worked with mostly terminally ill patients with cancer that, no matter what, would not survive their disease. They would be in the hospital for weeks at a time, going through a barrage of tests, getting chemotherapy, and then going home as an outpatient. But in a few weeks or months later, they would be back with the disease having gotten the best of them. They would have lost weight, had no hair on their scalps, and looked much sicker than they were when I last saw them. They always had a ray of hope that they would beat that dreaded disease, but I knew that unless a miracle occurred, for most of them, that was not going to happen.

The straw that broke the camel's back for me was an incident that happened one day while I was doing my injection rounds for the bone scan tests. Our department conducted a series of tests that were able to identify with great accuracy if the cancer had progressed, also known as metastasized, to other parts of the body. Even today, these tests are still carried out, but new procedures not available then, such as CAT, MRI, and PET scans, contribute much to a somewhat less painful series of tests. These tests are part of a terminology called a Metastatic Workup for cancer patients by physicians. Our lab procedures included bone, liver, and brain scans, and they are done over a week's span, one at a time. The test is usually painless other than the IV injection, but it requires the patient to hold still during many parts of the scan so that different views of that part of the body can be clearly imaged. As I made my rounds to give my injections early in the day in order to do the imaging later on, I entered a room where a nice older lady was lying in her bed. She was seventy-two years old, according to the physician consultation order that I had in my hands. The order said, "Please complete bone scan for metastatic workup. Patient has cancer that was discovered and resected nine months ago. Please compare with other bone scans." As I approached her, I introduced myself and told her that I was there to give her a small IV injection in one of her arms so that later on, in about three hours, we could do a bone scan in our lab. She must have been under some sedation because she responded slowly, but I proceeded to go ahead and look at the closer arm in order to locate a good vein. As soon as I touched her skinny, already bruised arm, probably from many other failed injections, she screamed that I was hurting her. I had just barely moved her arm slowly, a little bit out, and that caused pain. She said, "You're hurting me." I said, "Ma'am, where does it hurt?" She replied, "Everywhere that you touched." That was very unnerving for me. I had seen so many of these and I usually took all kinds of consideration before I attempted my injection. I said, "Ma'am, I am going to touch different bone areas in your body. Tell me where it hurts." I softly touched her shoulder close to her arm, and she screamed again. I then touched her upper chest; she screamed. The same thing happened when I touched her legs and the sides of her hip bones. Everything hurt her. I said, "Oh my God! This 100-pound human being has cancer in her bones almost everywhere I touch." I went out of her room and called my lab, and I asked the secretary, "What do we have on this patient as far as old tests?" She said, "Joe, she had two other metastatic workups in the last six months, including the bone scan." I asked her when we did the last bone scan, and she indicated that it was about ten weeks ago, and the one before that was five months ago. I asked her what we found on the previous scans, "She has metastatic bone cancer." I thanked her and hung up. I went through the patient's chart and saw that the woman was having all kinds of tests done to see if the chemotherapy was working. I said to myself, "I am going to stand up for this woman. She could be my grandmother. I do not want to put her through the bone scan. She would never hold still for me for those twenty minutes for the machine to scan her body. What a waste of time and energy, and putting her through that in her condition. What are these doctors trying to accomplish? You can medically observe that the cancer has now spread all over her bones." I looked at the order for the test and saw the doctor that ordered it, and I asked the nurse to page him for me. The nurse told me that he was the oncology resident but was not working currently and that the current doctor covering for him was there. I asked to speak with him instead. Within a couple of minutes, he calls in, and I get to speak with him after I identify myself. I communicated with him that we could not do the bone scan at this time on his patient. The reason was that I could not find a vein to inject her; additionally, she had bone pain everywhere I touched her plus, and because of that, she would not be able to hold still during our scan. I asked him, "Why are we repeating this bone scan for the third time again since the last one was done two and a half months ago, and we both know what that showed?" "Well," he said, "it is standard protocol to document her metastatic disease progress." I politely said, "I am sorry, but, unfortunately, we cannot do this procedure because of her pain status, including injecting her, if we can find a vein and get her to hold still for the duration of the scan. If this was even possible, you would have a technical substandard result that would not yield any good or additional information. We will put it on a waiting list pending her pain tolerance improving and due to our other time commitments. We have other patients that really do need a bone scan today. I will contact you on what day we can have a better time to get her test done and you let us know if she gets any better." I left that floor and continued to my last patient and went back to the lab. A couple of hours later, around lunch, the good old doctor, my chief, comes in "bow tie and all as usual," something out of the 1950s a Columbia medical school graduate, to spend the rest of the day at our hospital helping the other doctor to read the scans of the day with him. The phone rings in my department. I happened to take the call, and it was a doctor that identified himself as the resident for that older woman that I refused to do the bone scan for a couple of hours earlier. He asked to speak with the chief doctor that runs the lab. I was glad that the chief came in that day because I did not want the resident to speak with the other staff doctor. I asked him to hold on while I checked to see if the chief was available to take his call. I went over to his office and told him that a resident in oncology wanted to talk to him. I briefly explained the whole situation and what I told the attending physician about that patient; obviously, the resident didn't agree and wanted the test done anyway. I brought him the folder with all the other scans that she had, and I told him to review it while he talked to that guy. I left his office, but I said to him, "Doc, I just want you to know that this patient could be my grandmother, and I would not put her through this bone scan. If you read her chart like I did, you would see why. You tell this Resident the heck with protocols." I was not sure if the chief got my message. I was trying to say to let her live the rest of her days without being tortured any more by these doctors. They had given her their best shot, and like many others, the disease had progressed, and they failed. The chief came back to the lab and said to me, "Joe, I will do her scan," and I replied, "Doc, you have no clue how to run that machine." "Okay, Joe," he said, "you set everything up for me, and I will push the start button and be with her to get the bone scan done." "Great," I said, "you know what, Doc, go upstairs to her room in the oncology ward, and see her, and if you still want to do it, then good luck finding a vein to inject her with the radioisotope." He went up and twenty minutes later came back and said to me, "You were right. She hurt everywhere, but I tried to inject her, and her vein just broke. I couldn't do it." I replied, "Of course, with all the chemo that she has been getting, do you think you would find a vein that wouldn't bust and allow you to inject her?"

After that event, I realized that most doctors don't work for the well-being of their patients. Some of them are indoctrinated and taught to follow protocol and keep themselves out of a lawsuit. During all of those years, I saw many of those events where I said to myself "What am I doing here with these patients? Do you think I will help save their life?" Well, it was time for me to move on, and later that year, it happened. The chief retired, and I also left the hospital for more fertile grounds.

With the computer knowledge that I had acquired during my tenure at the hospital, I was able to get a job managing a local Radio Shack store and, later, a computer store. That was the closest that I could come to the computer world at that time. It was a far cry from what I had achieved at the hospital, and I also lost some of my personal status. I went back to Night College to learn additional things needed in the computer networking world. The first IBM personal computers were just hitting the market and when I finally sold a client one of those early systems, they didn't know how to use them in a practical way in their business. I decided to make some personal computer consulting business cards, and with that, I told potential clients that I could come to their business and teach them or their assistants how to use them. He asked me how much I charged, and I just shot a number out and asked, "Would twenty-nine dollars an hour be good for you?" He said, "Fine, come tomorrow and spend four hours at my office and see what we learn." I could not believe this! It was almost double what I used to make at the computer store. This was how I started my own computer consulting business while working at the computer store. Everyone was happy. The store would pay me for making the sale, and then I would personally make more, teaching the client how to use that computer. Within a year, I had several clients that would pay the same amount that I made in a week at the store, but I only had to work a little more than two days. "This is America," I said to myself. "You can write and make your own destiny if you have enough testicular fortitude; it is your choice." Entrepreneurship is what drives America. It allows someone witty with the knowledge to use it to the best of their abilities to bring rewards that are only limited by commitment and time.

It wasn't easy, especially for the first couple of years. I usually didn't get paid every week like I did at the hospital. Sometimes I had to wait several weeks for clients to pay, but when the checks finally arrived, they were sweet, and the amount was phenomenal. This is when I decided to rent a small office space and finally declared myself my own boss and business owner. A friend of my father by the name of Tony had just built a commercial building next to his cabinet-making shop. My father mentioned to me that he had a large empty room for rent in his new building that would be perfect for me as my new business office. From then on, I have been writing my own checks and still do today. The American dream was mine to take, and I didn't look back once. Every time I walked into my office, and that was not every day, I felt like a King. It was my own little kingdom, and nobody could take that away from me. I missed the pomposity that came with working at the hospital, but you know what, what I learned during those years is still well placed in me. So much that, when I go to see my current doctor for a medical visit, she says to me "Joe, today you are going to play the patient. Is that ok?" "Of course," I say to her, "I will be quiet and listen to your advice, but please remember that this is my body, and I only get one!" She laughs and says to me, "If you take your prescriptions, exercise, and follow my advice, you will live to be one hundred or maybe more." I said to her, "Thanks, Deborah. As long as you keep me out of any hospital, I am safe."

In the late eighties, I met a wonderful Italian woman, and I married her. We bought our own home shortly thereafter, and we have two beautiful and smart kids: a boy and a girl. My life, actually our life, was filled with many delightful God-given gifts, including the opportunity to earn a great living and share it with everyone that was around me.

My father, several years earlier, finally sold our old home and moved to a beautiful, larger, and newer home further out in the suburbs of Boston. That home had a country feel because of the large grassy yard with trees all around and a vegetable garden in the back. Everyone would gather at that home, and my mother would cook for everyone, especially on weekends, shared together with my sister's family and mine. It was nicknamed the Italian Villa by their neighbors because my father built a large cement deck attached to the back of the house thanks to his job and the cement trucks. Large pots of plants and flowers flourished all around, thanks to my mother's green thumb. My brother was the only one living with them now in that three-bedroom home. He also became a hairdresser, and when he wasn't at one of his girlfriends' homes, he would join us for those wonderful meals. He also had a nice habit of bringing his current girlfriend over to meet us, but, unfortunately, at his younger age, he would switch them out every few months. Everyone was welcomed at that house, and the gathering would often exceed twenty people. The large front driveway of this home would accommodate seven or eight cars comfortably. There was no need for anyone to park in the street. If it was too cold outside, then the finished basement of this house with its own fireplace was a beautiful setting for those winter nights and holidays.

My parents would travel to many vacation spots in the Caribbean now that only my brother was still living with them. My younger brother would keep an eye on the house while they were gone, so everything worked out fine. But Italy was always their favorite spot, even if it was not every year. I guess your homeland always has a special attraction. My father was now a senior mechanic at the cement-producing company. In fact, the workers had voted him to be their Union Shop Steward after they joined the "International Brotherhood of Teamsters" as "Machinists Local Union 25." This was the very union that Jimmy Hoffa was president of for almost fifteen years, and one day in 1975, he disappeared, and his body was never found.

MEMBER IDENTIFICATION CARD

Local Union No. 379

Boston Ma 02215-2077
CITY STATE ZIP CODE

AFFILIATED WITH THE
INTERNATIONAL BROTHERHOOD OF TEAMSTERS
CHAUFFEURS, WAREHOUSEMEN AND HELPERS OF AMERICA

Giorgio Galliani
NAME

026 42 7170 6/85
LEDGER NO. SOC. SEC. NO. INITIATED

SIGNATURE AND TITLE

Giorgio Galliani's Teamsters Member Identification Card.

Let's look at what my father achieved professionally over the years. He went from being an immigrant who spoke little English to being voted the union representative for the company, with one of the largest unions in the country. Why was my father put in that position? Well, when my father spoke, people listened. He wasn't afraid to say or tell you anything that he thought was important for management to be aware of. This is what we saw by reading about him during his work at the hydrofoil company in Messina, and things never changed with him no matter what country he was living in. His job was also very secure at the cement company. Where would they find another person that could rebuild those mighty diesel truck engines? When workers had grievances with management, they would go to him and say, "George, can you go fix this problem that we have here? By the way, we also need a pay raise!" Flexing the Teamster brand was a nice thing to use, but if he needed a helping hand getting the issues resolved, the local union president was always available to step in. Life was good, and as time went by, the respect from his co-workers and management increased exponentially. When he took three or four weeks off for a vacation, there was no discussion about it. He would leave plenty of refurbished engines behind, ready to be used as needed, and the company would have no reason to deny him that request since he had them covered.

It is now the 1990s. These were some of the best days of my life for both my father and me. My business was thriving on all cylinders, and my father was taking summer vacations to Italy with my mother, plus an additional week or two during the winter in the Caribbean. My mother recounted to me that during one of those vacations in Italy, my father reconnected with his old boss during a visit to the Cantieri Navali Rodriquez in Messina. This gentleman, Leopoldo "Duccio" Rodriguez, was now semi-retired, and the company had been going through radical changes for the last twenty-plus years. It was sold to other entities and was a much larger multi-operational company with different exposures and new additions. I believe he was just doing some consulting at that time for the company that his brother founded. Everyone was much older now. My father was approaching his sixtieth birthday, while Mr. Rodriquez was much older than him. But they both shared a long work history from when my father was employed by him. The Egyptian missions of the 1960s speak for themselves. I believe they started a beautiful relationship and began to share some great old memories. Mr. Rodriquez told my father that he came to America often because he had friends' doctors that would take care of his health requirements. I guess that speaks volumes about the American health system. He also told him that these doctors were located in the outskirts of Boston, in a town called Burlington, and that the hospital was called the Lahey Clinic. My father was astonished to hear that because that hospital was only ten minutes from his home! "Well," Mr. Rodriguez said to my father, "let me have your phone number, and on my next visit for a checkup there, I will call, and you and your lovely wife will be my guests for dinner." My father said, "Mr. Rodriquez, excuse my over-reach, but when you are in America, you are now in my country that I call home. I beg your pardon to ask you, but let me have the honor to be my guest for dinner at my home." "Giorgio," he said, "it would be my pleasure to be at your home and also meet your family." This was the beginning of a very interesting friendship that would last almost a decade. We will pick this up again as the years evolve and life takes its own course with twists and turns.

During the 1990s, my company really took off and it had nothing to do with the manner in which I was engaging potential clients, but rather in my way of carrying through with my father's traditions from what I learned growing up. He always told me when working for someone to "Always under promise and over deliver and then when you finally deliver, make sure that you always follow-up, to make sure they are happy with your work." I retained a couple of clients in the town where my office was located. The others were located in Boston and in a couple of surrounding towns. I hired an assistant to help me out with my paperwork and for purchasing the equipment. One of those local clients happened to be a small cooperative bank. I met a key person at the local Chamber of Commerce meeting that introduced me to their president, and that was a great business match. I helped them with their computer systems and lo and behold, I found out that they were holding in foreclosure a couple of beautiful condominiums from the last real estate debacle of the late 1980s. They had taken possession from the failed builder, and now they wanted to sell them and get them off their books. I was able to purchase probably the best penthouse in town from this client of mine, the bank. This is how, in an instant, my family was introduced to the ownership of a newly built home.

The price was negotiated for just about what I could afford, and they actually even gave me a mortgage on the property. This was a newly built, two-floor penthouse with spectacular views of Boston from the top floor. The circular spiral staircase was the "wow moment" that every one that came over to our new home recognized. It portrayed a touch of class reminiscent of an early real estate tycoon's penthouse.

Our first home, the penthouse with the spiral staircase and Jessica, my daughter.

As the years went by, I really executed a nice business venture and plan, but it was the word of mouth that brought in the most success. I would get a call saying, "I was told that you can supply us with computer systems, set them up for us, and also provide us with hands-on consulting." I would reply, "Yes, sir, and whom may I ask referred you to us?" "Well, your client so and so told me that I should call you. When can you come down and give us a proposal?" "I will be there tomorrow morning," I would say. That would be the start of a new beautiful, lasting, and profitable relationship. Then there was a state government client working on behalf of the City of Boston, again word of mouth, and also the Boston hospital EMS manager that needed specialized computers. Money was flowing in from all sides, and I was frequently out on sites. I had to personalize my services to meet each client's unique needs; this was my brand. I could not send my other tech; he would prepare the computers, but I would be the face of my company. It was not worth it to jeopardize that opportunity.

We lived comfortably in our penthouse during my daughter's early years. In 1993, my son, Giorgio, was born, and, unfortunately, the penthouse became unfeasible for a family of four, so we had to look for a new family home. The Dot.com days were fast approaching, but before then, an even bigger opportunity knocked on my door. A newly established startup company in the outskirts of Boston had a very innovative product that needed state-of-the-art, very fast personal computers. These machines were not to be used by people. Rather, they were connected in a large server room to do a particular job with each other, all in synch. These computers always had the same components inside without any deviation. The software that was tested on the initial unit could crash if the new batch of units was not exactly the same. The current vendor of those machines was a company that was trying to build its own brand and is now a Fortune 100 company. Their computers looked the same on the outside, but every month, they changed the inside components based on their sources. This was a problem for this client because they could not take a chance that some of these newer batch machines would crash in the middle of processing the data. The computer director of operations, "Harry," called one of his friends that happened to be buying computers from me and asked him, "Hey, do you have someone good and reliable that you have used to provide your company with fast and reliable computers?" He replied, "Yes, call Joe at his office and let him know your needs and requirements. I am sure he will be able to accommodate you." This was the beginning of a beautiful relationship with Harry and his company. This relationship went so well that we became close friends. I made him look like a hero at that company. You may not believe this, but we are still best friends even today. We both live in Florida and sometimes, when we talk about those old times, we wonder where those days have gone over one or two casual drinks.

With this value-added client revenue, I was able to put aside additional money. When an opportunity came to buy a nice brick home, I was able to pull the trigger and have my own villa, just like my father's, in the next town over. This home was a step up from his home, though. It included a heated in-ground pool for the kids, two kitchens, two living rooms, three bathrooms, and a grape pergola outside, and all located in a ritzy part of that town. Again, my life gets better and better every year for me, thanks to the opportunities given to everyone who works hard in this marvelous country called America.

During the final years before my father's retirement, he was not only going to Italy, but he would also spend a month during the winter season in a part of the world that he discovered through a friend. It was the Island of Margherita, located off the coast of Venezuela. He used to tell me that it reminded him so much of Tripoli. Many Italians lived there, and he rented a comfortable apartment on that island near the beachfront for the whole month. He would say to me, "Me and your mother go out several times a week to the restaurants with our friends and meet even more friends there." This vacation routine was his life for six or seven years, but this all was going to change when 2002 came around.

Let's go back to his relationship with Mr. Rodriquez to explain how life has a strange way of reaffirming itself. During one of their Italian vacations, Mr. Rodriguez invited my parents to his beautiful villa on the shores of Messina overlooking the strait. The occasion was to celebrate the wine harvesting season. The villa was located on a large family plot of land where there were many vines of grapes, olive trees, and fruit trees. During the wine harvesting season, Mr. Rodriquez would hire some of the local help to pick the grapes and bring them to the part of the house where the wine was made in his cantina. It was wonderful to see how an individual coming from a different social class recognized my father's hard work with admiration in establishing this beautiful friendship. Both men were now enjoying some well-deserved leisure time after a lifetime of hard work and professional achievements. Who could have imagined this future scenario during our previous life in Messina? People would say that we were crazy.

Mr. Rodriquez received a kidney transplant in the 1990s in Boston. Every year, he would travel to see his doctors in Massachusetts for routine tests to make sure that all was well. But now, with this new-found relationship with my father, his visits have become less stressful and a bit easier to endure. My father would make arrangements for him to stay at a nearby hotel when he flew in, and my parents would invite the couple to their home. While we did not have any grapes at my father's villa, my mother's homemade dinner was a favorite for them, together with great conversation following coffee and dessert. During those years, I had the privilege to be there a few times.

My mother would call the elder couple the day before to see what they preferred to eat since Mr. Rodriquez and his wife were on modified diets. My mother always placed me across the table from Mr. Rodriquez. She would sit across from his wife, while my father would be seated in the middle at the head of the table. We would engage in intellectual talks about the current technology trends, which Mr. Rodriguez really enjoyed. When it was my opportunity to ask questions, I would always ask him about the hydrofoils, about the current company, and those old golden times. Maybe I always knew that I was going to write a book where he would be part of it. I couldn't take my eyes off Mr. and Mrs. Rodriguez's gorgeous matching Rolex watches. I still don't own one myself, even if I could. I have a thin wrist, and that work of art might stand out as too flashy for me.

In any case, back at the dinner table, I always took the initiative in speaking with Mr. Rodriguez. I felt that my father, even though Mr. Rodriquez highly respected him at this point, would only inject his thoughts as an addition to our discussions. I felt that my father still maintained a state of mind that he was still the employee and Mr. Rodriquez was still his boss. That was my father's old-fashioned thinking and personality, sitting next to one of the owners of the Cantieri Navali Rodriquez, a pioneer in that field. I would tend to my father's shyness with my conversational engagements. In my computer business, I always dealt with influential people. I wanted my father to also feel important. "Yes, Dad, you are a really accomplished father. Look around you. Everything and everyone is here because of you." I would have loved for him to stand up and raise the glass of wine many times and say to everyone there, "Let's raise our wine glass in a toast to our guests, that we may enjoy their company for a very long time. Cheers." No, my father was not that kind of person. I am because I was the new generation of entrepreneurs. I became a business person by dealing with other business persons; it was a routine that I carried out every day and still do to a lesser degree today thirty-five years later.

Mr. Rodriquez was intrigued by what I did for work when we first met. When I told him about my medical background and then my computer company, I think he raised an eyebrow as if to say "A successful father leads to a more successful son." Not necessarily. I am not a pioneer or a magnate like Mr. Rodriquez. I am someone that reached for the stars and ended up with a piece of the moon. Not many people can say that they achieved that all on their own. It takes respect, resilience, perseverance, hard work, and sometimes a little bit of luck.

When my father reached his retirement age, he could not wait to stop working. When he finally did in 1997, he left the concrete company by telling them, "I am retiring now. Here is my thirty days' notice." Management begged him to stay part-time and rebuild at least one engine a month, and they would pay him even more for his time. But he wouldn't budge a bit. Does this sound familiar? Yes! Remember when Mr. Rodriquez asked him <u>not</u> to immigrate to America and stay with the company while offering him a nice salary increase? He said then, and this was still in play, "When I make up my mind, nothing will change it." This also was the case with the trucking company. He was leaving for good, and he wasn't coming back. My father had been working non-stop since he was sixteen, as you will recall from the Tripoli days. He just wanted to sleep in the morning, enjoy his yard, and work on his cars if he felt like it. There was no more punching the time card in the morning and then again in the afternoon. He just wanted to be free and enjoy the retirement he had earned and more. He had reached pension status with the union, collected social security, and also received a small Italian pension. He could travel more, visit different Caribbean islands, the Island of Margarita, and not worry about coming back. My mother was not always on-board because she wanted to take care of my sister's kids, but she always went along.

When Mr. Rodriquez visited, he was now free to go with him around town. He was in Boston every year, and sometimes twice a year now, because his transplanted kidney was starting to fail. By the year 2000, he was put on a waiting list to receive a new kidney at the Lahey Clinic. My father alleviated some of his travel needs, as usual, by making sure that the hotel room was reserved and ready for his arrival. I remember my mother making sure that they had basic food and drinks in their room's refrigerator when they arrived so that they did not need to go to the market.

The Dot.com days came and went. Many people made fortunes while others lost them. The internet brought in a new way to communicate with people and places, and I was there from the very beginning with the first IBM personal computer that I used to sell. I remember one day in the 1980s; we delivered an original IBM Dual floppy machine to an important early client. When the machine booted up, it came up with A:>PCDoS. My assistant, a much younger kid, said to me, "Boss, why are you giving these guys PCDos?" I replied, "They bought a real IBM. What should I give them?" He said, "Boss, me and you know that MSDos is much better, faster, occupies less memory, and has many more options." I replied, "Why would I give them Microsoft Dos? Who are they? IBM will eat them alive. They will be gone by next year." "Fine," he said, "this is why you're the boss, and I am just helping you." I should have listened to the kid and bought one hundred shares of Microsoft and put them away. It was 1984, and I sure hope he did! When the year 2000 came, the world did not come to an end as many people had predicted. We made a lot of money upgrading computers that could not handle the year 2000 clock. They did not even ask us how much it cost.

Life was moving along at warp speed for me. My two kids were growing up so fast. The new millennium brought in a bit of a midlife crisis for me. Luckily, my business did not suffer the same fate. I was just sailing through. I did not want to expand my business or make it bigger. After all, I wanted to sleep at night. Every one of my clients loved me, and they trusted me with their technology platform which was what kept them in business. None of them ever complained about paying too much or asked why they needed to buy new equipment. All I had to say to them was: "I am looking out for you, and I don't want you to call me one morning to say, 'My servers at one of my remote sites or computer room are down.'" The standard reply was, "Joe if you think we need a new one, get it done. Our computers have become far too important for us." So, life continued trending along quite nicely.

In 2002, two important events occurred that sent a curve ball to my father. One of them would turn out to be really pleasant, while the other would put an end to one of his personal legacies. I will bring the positive one into perspective first. I must give credit to my younger brother, Vincenzo because he made it happen. He had more time than all of us to lead this venture because he was a single man and remains the everlasting bachelor today.

My parents were vacationing every year in Margherita Island off the coast of Venezuela. Unfortunately, that location was out of easy reach for all of us to go visit them. It was just too far and too complicated to get there. My brother had traveled to Florida many times in the late 1990s and early 2000s. He finally convinced my father to take a look at Florida as an alternative vacation spot. My father had his own vision of Florida: the snakes, alligators, and bugs, but that was far from reality. Florida was fast becoming the number one state for retirees. In early 2001, he persuaded me and my mother to go on a short trip there just to check things out and to show them around Florida. When they arrived, they liked what they saw, and it was not anywhere near what they had imagined. To make things even more appealing, it was a short three-hour flight from Boston as opposed to the complicated Margherita trek. Florida is part of America. What you see in

Boston is also in Florida: the same chain stores, the English-speaking restaurants, but more importantly, the people. Why would they want to vacation in a foreign country?

During their visit, they came across several new real estate developments that would be ready to be occupied within the next year. One of these complexes stood out more than the others to them. It was an over 55 community in a tranquil and well-planned town in Palm Beach County. Homes in this complex were currently being pre-sold with scaled-down models of all the homes available to be seen in the builder's sales office. Thanks to my brother's diligence, my parents agreed to put a deposit on a new villa, and, with a bit of help from me and him, the deal was done. I really never saw my father happier than when he flew back to Boston and told me about his purchase. He looked like he had just acquired heaven. He would talk about it all the time from then on while he was keeping track of the building progress. He looked to me like a child that had candy in his mouth all the time.

In early 2002, the home was completed, and now my father was the proud owner of a large two-bedroom Florida Villa with two baths plus an extra room for more guests. I believe that the juices of his American dream were flowing through every vein of his body reinvigorating his now seventy plus years. What an accomplishment, Dad! Now he even had a winter home in Florida, just like many people dream about. My father had already sold both of his homes in Italy a while back and the money was in the bank awaiting this final opportunity. This is what retirement is all about and what America can offer to everyone that works hard, lives a respectful life, and plays by her rules.

My parents' new winter home in Florida with an indoor garage.

Come winter 2002, our clan collectively spent little time in Boston. Instead, we enjoyed a brand-new fresh-smelling seventeen-hundred-square-foot villa in southeastern Florida. Our families and our young kids could not wait to go visit their grandparents in that new Florida home. It was so easy to get there by plane, and my father would be there at the airport to pick all of us up. We would leave the cold days of the Boston winter behind to stay in the warm Florida climate. When we were there, we were out every day, going to the nearby beach, walking around the local stores, and eating gelato in the middle of the Boston winter. Everyone was really happy to finally have a home where it counts in the winter. Spending time with my parents and also with my kids during the winter school vacation week was a blessing for everyone. That is life and what dreams are made of because we used to see it only on TV in the past.

My father became a real fan of Florida. All the things that he had assumed were only a product of his imagination. Florida life was quite nice and different, and he loved it. My father now owned two villas: one in Boston and one in Florida, and he earned them fairly and squarely. My father was seventy years young and was enjoying life to its fullest. He deserved it, and all of us were always watching his back.

Around that time, Mr. Rodriquez was notified that a new kidney was available at the hospital near my parents' home in Boston. As usual, my father catered to his usual accommodation needs before their arrival. He was going to have a surgical transplant procedure and that was not a walk in the park. It was always my pleasure to spend quality time with Mr. Rodriquez during those memorable Galliani family dinners.

Unfortunately, things did not go well for Mr. Rodriguez during the transplant operation. He ended up in the intensive care unit, which was unexpected. Several days went by, and he was not getting better. The doctors were optimistic that he would eventually make it through because he was a strong man. I don't know what happened, but his immediate family decided to pick him up in a private jet and bring him back to Italy, where he passed away a few days later. We were all very saddened by the course of those events. He had become a close family friend that we looked forward to spending time with. I think my father was very much affected by this event. Mr. Rodriquez was much older than my father, but I guess he also experienced a reality check that he also wasn't a young guy anymore. The death of Mr. Rodriquez brought the final closure to my father's old professional experiences and memories that started such a long time ago, in the early 1960s. I believe it must have been a great ride for him. Even more amazing was at the end of it all; he had reconnected so closely with his ex-boss. This is truly one of the great miracles of the circle of life.

I believe that after that event, my father got a dose of truth. He decided it was now the time to live an even fuller life without any more hurdles. He was in Florida anytime he could get away from Boston, not only in the winter but also a few times in the summer and fall. His perception was that when he was there, his mind was free to find that absolute tranquility that always had eluded him. My mother even allowed him to go there alone because she was busy taking care of my sister's two young boys. Being self-employed, I also had the flexibility to travel there when I could get away from my work in Boston. So, a few times, it was just me and him at the Florida Villa talking and going out on the avenue where all the shops and restaurants were located. I must also say that my father was a great cook, and he rather liked to eat dinner at home. In the morning, he would ask me what I wanted to eat that night. He would get in the car during the day and drive over to a nearby Italian market and buy everything that we needed. This reminded me of life as a young boy when my mother used to send me to the local food store when we lived in Messina. How wonderful it is to see how life almost repeats itself, not exactly the same, but with a vengeance to bring back old memories. Those dinners with just the two of us in his Florida home will always be wonderful memories for me. Regrettably, we didn't talk too much about personal matters, but now, in retrospect, we should have. He could have helped me to mitigate some of my personal problems. We mostly discussed the news events of the day; then, he would retire early for the night because he loved to get up early and cook breakfast for both of us. For my part, after dinner, I used to go out to the avenue, where many people gathered, for a well-deserved cocktail. During the winter, many people that were in town from New England spent their cold months in this part of southern Florida. I always asked them, when I had the opportunity to exchange a conversation, why they were in Florida. Their answer pretty much matched that of my father. It really was "The Sunshine State" and a slice of paradise.

That year, my company was awarded a contract from a well-known hospitality group to install wireless internet access at some of their hotels along the eastern coast of the United States. My company was always on top of the latest technology, and wireless internet, or Wi-Fi was becoming well-adopted as a means to connect to the internet for business travelers staying in hotels. I don't recall the exact location, but in late 2004, I was in the Tampa, Florida, area to install the wireless infrastructure at one of these hotels. I was able to accomplish my work ahead of schedule, and I decided to drive to the east coast because my father was at his house for one of his non-winter visits. When I called him to let him know that I would drive and stay with him for a couple of days, he was very excited to have me there on this unplanned trip. He told me that if I would be there by 6:00 PM, he would have dinner ready for us. My favorite meal was homemade sauce and spaghetti with fried eggplant on top of it. He was planning on making that since that was also his favorite.

When I arrived just before dinner time, he had everything ready, simmering on the stove, just like my mother used to do for him when he would come home late from work in Messina decades ago. I hugged him when I saw him like I used to do when I was very young when he walked in the front door at our Messina home. We had a nice bottle of wine with the spaghetti meal, an espresso, and also some fresh pastries that he bought for us. I had the nightly Jägermeister that he always had in the freezer for me, and we both went to bed early that night. I was also tired from the three-hour drive across Florida.

The guest bedroom was located all the way on the other side of the Villa. This made guests always feel like they had their own private space, which included their own private bathroom. During that night, I heard my father coughing most of the time, so much so that he kept me up at the opposite side of the home. I was not sure if he actually realized that he had these frequent coughing events. The next morning, I spoke to him and asked him if he realized that he coughed a lot when he was lying down in bed sleeping. He said that it had been happening for the last few months, but it went away when he got up. I recalled my medical days at the hospital. When a patient was supine, it triggered that kind of cough if there was fluid in the lungs. I asked him to please see the doctor that he had in Florida and get a chest X-ray on Monday since it was the weekend. I told him that I had to go back to Boston on Monday morning and that I would call him at night to find out what the doctor said. Well, when I got back to my office on Monday afternoon, I could not wait to speak to him and see how everything went. Instead of getting a call from him, I received a call from his doctor late that day, around 5:00 PM. He must have given him my phone number. I distinctly recall this doctor introducing himself to me. He identified himself as his primary care doctor for my father when he was in Florida and said that my father asked him to let me know about the chest x-ray if everything was ok. This was the most devastating call of my life because, as a medically experienced person, I could read between the lines of his conversation. The doctor told me that, indeed, my father had fluid in both lungs. He said that it didn't look like pneumonia to him because his lungs also had diffused spots all over them. Regrettably, he said that further tests would need to be done to evaluate what the X-ray was really showing. But, he privately shared his opinion with me: "I want your father to go see a lung specialist as soon as he comes back to Boston. Mr. Galliani," he said, "I have seen a lot of these X-rays in my life. I want to let you know that, hopefully, I am wrong, but those images do not look good to me. I wish you and your father much luck, and hopefully, I will see him again on his next trip here."

My father came back to Boston a couple of days later, and the first thing that we did was to take him directly to the hospital near his house. This was the same hospital where Mr. Rodriquez was a patient for the last decade for his kidney transplants. A CAT scan and an analysis of the lungs' fluid was performed. Both tests confirmed that my father had the worst imaginable disease. He was diagnosed with Stage 4 diffuse small cell lung cancer. That diagnosis was a crushing reality for me and for everyone else in my family. We communicated to him that they found a type of cancer but that the doctors felt that they could stop it in its tracks and get him to feel better soon.

But I knew what that diagnosis really meant. I had seen it hundreds of times before during my nuclear medicine years. It was a death sentence that could not be rendered inoffensive. If it had already spread, it would probably breach his other organs.

The family decided to bring him to the downtown Boston hospital that specialized in this type of cancer. The results and opinions there were not much different. We decided to try to see if chemotherapy would at least slow down the cancer to give him a little more time. I believe that the drug had the opposite effect. It seemed that it accelerated its growth and his symptoms. The metastatic workup test that I described so well during my nuclear medicine tenure showed that the cancer had also spread to his bones. It was very sad to see a strong, healthy man deteriorate so fast in front of your eyes. In a few short months, three to be exact, the disease ravished my father's body. While my father was not a religious man, as you may recall from our years living in Messina, he had a strong Catholic sense of morality. In his deeply sedated state, we arranged for the local priest to come administer the Viaticum, better known as the Last Rites. On December 21, 2004, he died quietly at his home in the early morning hours, with many of us around him. The train of life had finally reached its destination, and my father had to step out to hopefully reach a better life after death.

He was buried in a local Catholic cemetery in the northern Boston suburb where he lived. The gravestone has a picture of him with an inscription saying "Caro Amato Marito e Padre," which translates to "Dear Beloved Husband and Father." Life was changed for everyone in my family after his death. My mother tried to get everyone to be as we were before, but the Christmases, New Year's, and Easter's lost their gleam without him. For my part, I was able to give some meaning to my future and patch things up, but it was very hard. This was thanks partially to my twelve-year-old son, Giorgio, and my sixteen-year-old daughter, Jessica. Even if they missed their grandfather on those special occasions, they developed the Galliani mental fortitude. As my doctor always said to me, "You can't beat your genes. It is your etched life and is part of who we are."

I spent the next sixteen years after his death finding meaning and a way to attempt to be who he was. I must say that those were very big shoes to fill. The times have changed, and who I am is not what I really hoped to be. My legacy is going to be much different than that of what my father was. Both of my kids are doing very well. With me and their mother by their side, they turned out to be an integral part of American society. Their college education and Italian culture have survived the test of time, and they are now part of conservative America. With this book and its content, I don't want to give myself that much credit. I can still remember that when my father was present, and he called them, for whatever reason, my kids just dropped everything and listened to what he had to say. All of us will always silently carry his persona and ideas to make us better human beings.

Seven years ago, I was also able to execute my dream of living in a part of America that closely resembles my early years in Messina. I left the cold climate of the Northeast and found my way to Florida, just like him. The weather is very much like that of Sicily and sometimes, during those hot days, I can still daydream about my lazy hot afternoons on that balcony in our little home in Messina. Having my son here in Florida is a comfort, and hopefully, my daughter eventually, will also join me. As I have cut down on my IT business over the last few years, I found the time to write this book. I thought it was going to be an easy task, but this was the hardest thing that I was ever faced with. My life and story continue today, hopefully, to teach my kids what it takes to get there as a better person. They need to recognize why we are all here, how we found our way here, and who that pioneer was that made everyone's life what it is today. Every day that I wake up, especially on a lazy, bright sunny day, I take the time to think about those fond memories of my father's trek around the world. I think he would have enjoyed this life, my life, if he was here for a little bit longer because I believe he deserved it and worked a lot harder than me. Unfortunately, the time came for him to move on to a better place and leave what he had established behind for our enjoyment. I will always keep him in my thoughts and strive every day to be what he always taught me to be. He was that person who many people who met him throughout the world thought, "He can walk on water."

My current Florida home. It is not Sicily, but on lazy, hot summer afternoons, I can sometimes feel in the air a bit of my Father's soul.

EPILOGUE

When my father died suddenly, much too young, he took his vision and also ours, at least temporarily, with him. When a family loses their leader that has set a tone for everyone's life for over half a century, a void is created. The family members, even if they now have their own family, are very much affected in their daily life. My father's loss was just overwhelming, and nobody could ever take his place. The only options were to try to convey his lifestyle, and to learn from his teaching and legacy. We had nobody left to look up to, to give us advice, or to call. When sheep lose their Shepherd, they become disoriented and wander around without guidance. This was me and our family when my father was no longer there. We felt that we could not find our way back to a normal life. This book has given me a way to reflect on my life, in recounting his, mine, that of others, and of everyone that modified my persona, hopefully, to finally find my way back. It has given me a sense of direction for my accomplishments, maybe not on the same scale as his, but at least in a way to bring some closure to his legacy. In sharing our rich past and history through this book to anyone that is captivated, may you learn what it takes to become relevant in your life with your family and your friends. All of us, because of his teachings and past presence, have learned to make each day a day to remember. Always try to make a difference with a passion and whatever that may bring out in you to make you a better person. If you do it right, for enough time, and for the right reasons, maybe someday someone will say the same about you: "*I think that individual could walk on water.*"

I know I can definitely say that about my father. *I am not sure if my kids or anyone else will say that about me. We will leave that to the future to decide.*

And for you all, the readers, and your last evaluation: Did the American immigration laws of our past accomplish the correct results? Did this book make you reflect on your disposition toward America's current immigration method? I am confident that my family was one of many legal immigrants who respected, assimilated, integrated, collaborated, and participated in the grandiose worldly stand that America hopefully portrays today. Finally, was my father "The Last Real Immigrant?"

Joseph

ACKNOWLEDGMENTS

The person that inspired this book was my mentor, my father, Giorgio Galliani! May we meet once again! Your incredible life story, our story, is now for everyone to read and enjoy!

Special thanks to my mother, and to my aunts Maria and Anna in Italy, for telling me our history before I came to be.

To my contributor and editor, Kristen Queenan, who spent countless hours in conversations, editing, and scouring this book by making these writings a runway red carpet for the inner me.

This book is also dedicated to all of the wonderful people that have been part of my life. Especially all those beautiful Italian women that have crossed my path. Every one of them left some lasting inspiration in my soul to push the limits of my imagination. Especially to the one that is still here!

To the many friends that supported me on this project, by just being there and listening to me for the last several years. There were times when I gave up, but they said take some time off, you will see, it will come back to you. They were right; it eventually did.

To Mr. John Ermilio, my first editor: "*You have a story to tell.*"

Special thanks to Cosmo for his final help.

I also want to express "Thanks" to all those who were less invigorating with their interactions. It made me even more unwavering and gave me that extra strength needed to move forward and accomplish this mystical undertaking.

Finally, I leave this book as a legacy for my family. Especially when seeking some kind of truth or perspective to what drove this guy - Me - for the better but sometimes for the worse. It is part of being human to have faults, but if you trouble yourself to look behind them, you might discover and unfold some well-hidden talents and merits.

Now you know who I am!

"non si vive un'altra volta"
"você não vive de novo"
"you don't live again"
"no vives de nuevo"

CPSIA information can be obtained
at www.ICGtesting.com
Printed in the USA
LVHW051533240723
753302LV00032B/192/J

9 781961 074019